Catastrophic Thinking

Catastrophic Thinking

Ben Shapiro

Creators Publishing
Hermosa Beach, CA

CATASTROPHIC THINKING
Copyright © 2020 CREATORS PUBLISHING
All rights reserved. No part of this book may be reproduced or transmitted in any form or by any means, electronic or mechanical, including photocopying, recording or by any information storage and retrieval system, without permission in writing from the author.

Cover art by Peter Kaminski

CREATORS PUBLISHING
737 3rd St
Hermosa Beach, CA 90254
310-337-7003

Although the author and publisher have made every effort to ensure that the information in this book was correct at press time, the author and publisher do not assume and hereby disclaim any liability to any party for any loss, damage or disruption caused by errors or omissions, whether such errors or omissions result from negligence, accident or any other cause.

ISBN (print): 978-1-949673-26-5
ISBN (ebook): 978-1-949673-25-8

First Edition
Printed in the United States of America
1 3 5 7 9 10 8 6 4 2

A Note From the Publisher

Since 1987, Creators has syndicated many of your favorite columns to newspapers. In this digital age, we are bringing collections of those columns to your fingertips. This will allow you to read and reread your favorite columnists, with your own personal digital archive of their work.
—Creators Publishing

Contents

2019: The Year of the Wokescolds	1
The Scientific Experts Who Hate Science	4
When Checks and Balances Fail	7
Factually Incorrect Cannot Be Morally Correct	9
The Democrats' Radicalism Problem	11
Baby Killing Is Fine. Yearbook Photos Are the Problem	13
The Republican Pouncing Problem	15
3 Lessons From the Jussie Smollett Hoax	17
Venezuela and the Myth of Kinder, Gentler Socialism	19
The Righteous Mission of Bernie Sanders	22
Government Isn't the Social Fabric	24
How to Silence Debate, New Zealand Edition	26
Why We Don't Trust Our Institutions?	28
When You Don't Appreciate Your Civilization	31
The Open Borders Agenda Rears Its Ugly Head	33
Criticism of Ilhan Omar Isn't Incitement	35
Can Joe Biden Apologize His Way to the Presidency?	37
Why Scorn Matters	39
The Manufactured Constitutional Crisis	41
No, Abortion Isn't a Constitutional Right	43
Why We Can Learn From the European Union	45
Why Celebrity Politics Matters	47
The Media/Democrat Complex Strikes Big Tech	49
Freedom From Consequences Isn't Freedom	52
Anger for Anger's Sake	55
The News Cycle Without Trump's Tweets	58
Why the Left Is Reconsidering Al Franken	61
Baltimore, Land of Political Footballs	63
Why Can't We Unify in the Face of Evil?	65
Why We Embrace Conspiracy Theories	67
The Media's Intersectional Embrace of Anti-Semitism	70
Trump Is Right on the China Threat	73

How the Quest for Power Corrupted Elizabeth Warren	75
Did We Learn the Lesson of 9/11?	78
The Alternative History of the United States	80
Catastrophic Thinking Without Solutions	85
Impeachment Isn't Merited	85
The NBA Proves The Corporate Social Activism Is All About the Dollars	87
Beto Says the Quiet Part out Loud	90
The 'Lynching' Controversy and the Death of Common Language	92
The J Street Democrats	95
Is Elizabeth Warren Set to Fall?	98
Are Conservative Immigration Restrictionists Racists?	100
How to Disunite America	102
Pete Buttigieg's Big Mistake: Telling the Truth	104
The Disproportionate Trickle-Down of Bad Social Politics	107
Will Democrats Accept Results of the 2020 Elections?	110
The Right to Destroy Cities	112
About the Author	114

2019: The Year of the Wokescolds

January 2, 2019

2018 was a chaotic year. It was a chaotic year for the markets, for domestic and international politics, and for social mores. 2019 promises more of the same, if the end of the prior year was any indicator. And it promises something else: the continued rise of the Wokescolds.

Wokescolds are the new representatives of moral panic. We've seen plenty of moral panic before in the United States, from worries about violent video games, to concern about allegations of sex abuse at day care facilities. But never have we seen a moral panic of the stunning breadth of today's woke moral panic. It's a moral panic that insists we change fundamental characteristics of our society, from biology, to language, to politics, to religion, to romantic relations, to art, to comedy.

We're told that if we fail to rewrite biology to suggest there are more than two sexes, or if we don't use preferred pronouns rather than biological ones, we will inevitably create emotional and mental instability among certain vulnerable groups. We're told that if we fail to silence members of groups who haven't suffered sufficiently in the United States, we will be contributing to the perpetuation of power hierarchies that target minorities. We're told that if we don't force religious people to violate their own standards in order to cater to those engaging in what they consider to be sinful activity, we will be bolstering religious oppression. We're told that the only proper type of sexual relationship is one initiated via contractual levels of affirmative consent, rather than mere affirmative body language or acquiescence. We're told that "Baby, It's Cold Outside" and "The Philadelphia Story" are deeply troubling hallmarks of our sexist past (modern rap, replete with brutal degradation of women, is just fine, in case you were wondering). And we're told that if we consider politically incorrect jokes funny, we're strengthening regressive stereotypes.

If we fail to abide by these new strictures, we will be attacked by the Wokescolds. These "woke" inquisitors have apparently mastered the ever-shifting dynamics of leftist power politics and are willing to scour everyone's online history and interpersonal relationships for signs of heresy. Once such heresy is uncovered, the Wokescolds truly go to work: They demand apologies from the supposed sinners and boycotts of those who refuse to disassociate from them. They discourage decent people from speaking up—better to stay silent so as to avoid the wrath of the Wokescolds.

The Wokescolds deliberately pick marginal cases—cases on which good people may be split. This allows the Wokescolds to consistently narrow the boundaries of safety for those who disagree with them.

The latest victim of the Wokescolds: Louis C.K. Now, C.K. has a reprehensible personal history; by his own admission, he used his position of fame and power to lure up-and-coming female comedians backstage, where he would then ask them to watch him touch himself. C.K. has apologized for that behavior. But now he's back on the road, and he's beginning to make jokes again.

This must not be allowed, particularly when his jokes are about such taboo topics as gender pronouns and the alleged expertise conferred by experiencing tragedy. And so C.K. has been pronounced Unwoke. See, before his #MeToo moment, he was sufficiently politically leftist to avoid the Wokescold wrath—after all, he once called Sarah Palin a "c---." But now, C.K. must pay the price for not being sufficiently woke. Those who watch his comedy must be shamed. And we must suggest that he is no longer Funny.

Now, the difference between being funny and being Funny is that when you're funny, everyone knows it—when you're Funny, as defined by critics, you don't have to be funny. You just have to be woke, like the awfully unfunny Hannah Gadsby. *Real humor* requires only satisfying the Wokescolds. We've all just been misdefining comedy for a few millennia.

If all this sounds dull, obnoxious and frustrating, that's because it is. And while the Wokescolds may win temporary victories, those victories will surely be Pyrrhic: As it turns out, we tend to like our biology, language, politics, religion, romantic relationships, art and comedy. The Wokescolds will certainly lose. But not before they destroy a *lot* of people and fray the social fabric nearly beyond repair.

The Scientific Experts Who Hate Science

January 9, 2019

This week, the American Psychological Association proved once again that it is a political body rather than a scientific one. This isn't the first time a major mental health organization has favored politics over science—in 2013, the American Psychiatric Association famously reclassified "gender identity disorder" in the Diagnostic and Statistical Manual of Mental Disorders, calling it "gender dysphoria" and then explaining that living with the delusion that you are a member of the opposite sex is not actually a mental disorder at all. That ruling was based on *zero* scientific evidence—much like the original DSM-5 classification of pedophilia as a "sexual orientation" before it was renamed "pedophilic disorder" under public pressure.

The latest example of the American Psychological Association's political hackery concerns the topic of "traditional masculinity." In the APA journal, it announced that it had released new guidelines to "help psychologists work with men and boys." Those guidelines suggest that "40 years of research" show that "traditional masculinity is psychologically harmful and that socializing boys to suppress their emotions causes damage that echoes both inwardly and outwardly." The APA explains that "traditional masculinity—marked by stoicism, competitiveness, dominance and aggression—is, on the whole, harmful. Men socialized in this way are less likely to engage in healthy behaviors."

Never mind that traditional masculinity—a masculinity geared toward channeling masculine instincts of building and protecting, rather than tearing down—built Western civilization and protected it from the brutalities of other civilizational forces. Never mind that traditional masculinity protected femininity and elevated women to equal status in public policy. Traditional masculinity is actually just men sitting around and eating burgers while grunting at one another about football, all the while crying on the inside because they have been prohibited by society from showing their feelings.

And it's worse than that. According to the APA, traditional masculinity bumps up "against issues of race, class and sexuality," maximizing both interior and exterior conflict. Dr. Ryon McDermott, a psychologist from the University of South Alabama who helped draft the new APA guidelines, suggested that gender is "no longer just this male-female binary." Rather, gender is a mere social construct that can be destroyed without consequence. Here's the APA making the extraordinarily dishonest statement that gender differences aren't biological *at all*, in contravention of all known social science research: "Indeed, when researchers strip away stereotypes and expectations, there isn't much difference in the basic behaviors of men and women."

Destroy masculinity in order to destroy discrimination and depression. Feminize men, and indoctrinate boys.

In order to reach this conclusion, the APA has to define traditional masculinity in the narrowest, most negative terms possible—and then other those who disagree as part of the patriarchy. But as a political body, the APA has little problem doing this.

All of this is not only nonsense; it's wildly counterproductive nonsense. Buried beneath the reams of nonsense in the APA report is this rather telling gem: "It's also important to encourage pro-social aspects of masculinity. ... In certain circumstances, traits like stoicism and self-sacrifice can be absolutely crucial." But we must never suggest that such traits ought to be included as part of a "traditional masculinity," because that would make some people feel excluded.

Here's the truth: Men are looking for meaning in a world that tells them they are perpetuators of discrimination and rape culture; that they are beneficiaries of an overarching, nasty patriarchy; that they are, at best, disposable partners to women, rather than protectors of them. Giving men purpose requires us to give them purpose *as men*, not merely as genderless beings. There's a lot to be said for the idea that our culture has ignored the necessity for men to become gentlemen. But that's a result of a left-wing culture that denigrates men, not a traditional masculinity built on the idea that men were born to defend, protect and build.

One thing is certainly true, though: The APA has destroyed itself on the shoals of politics. And there's no reason for honest-thinking people to take its anti-scientific pronouncements seriously simply because it masquerades as scientists while ignoring facts in favor of political correctness.

When Checks and Balances Fail

January 16, 2019

In February 2017, Dr. Christopher Duntsch became the first surgeon in American history known to be sentenced to prison for botching a patient surgery. A licensed neurosurgeon, Duntsch left a string of deaths and maimed bodies in his wake: He was accused of causing the death of two surgery patients and leaving 33 others permanently damaged. His patients left their lives in his hands; he left them paralyzed or dead.

The checks and balances that were supposed to contain Duntsch failed utterly. His medical school licensed him but didn't require the preparation necessary to instill competence. Hospitals suspended him but didn't report him. The medical board could do nothing without forms filed against him. Patients were left without recourse.

When checks and balances fail, damage is usually the result.

That's why when it came to our system of government, the founders were so focused on creating gridlock. They recognized that in a system in which legitimacy sprang from popular support, the easy path to perdition lay in popularly backed centralized power—tyranny could spring just as easily from a popular majority as from a king or despot. The founders didn't trust individuals with authority, and they didn't trust human beings to delegate authority to mere individuals.

But popular governments have always bucked against such limitations.

The majority of Americans always want action, on some grounds or others. That leads to an eternal drive to grant unchecked power to some institution of government. As Alexis de Tocqueville writes in his 1840 "Democracy in America": "It may easily be foreseen that almost all the able and ambitious members of a democratic community will labor without ceasing to extend the powers of government, because they all hope at some time or other to wield those powers. ... Centralization will be the natural government."

We're now seeing the consequences of such centralization on two separate fronts: the president's authority to declare a national emergency and the FBI's investigations into the president. Proponents of President Trump would like to see power centralized in the presidency; antagonists of President Trump would like to see power centralized in the FBI.

President Trump's allies seem eager for Trump to declare a national emergency in order to appropriate funds for a border wall. The law cuts against such a declaration: The National Emergencies Act was written to curtail presidential authority, not increase it. No matter how much border hawks (including me) want a border barrier, the proper method is to request funds from Congress.

Meanwhile, President Trump's enemies are celebrating reports this week that the FBI investigated Trump as a possible Russian agent after his firing of then-FBI director James Comey. Trump had authority under the Constitution to fire Comey, and there's no actual evidence that Trump is an agent of the Russians. But Trump's enemies want the legislature to step in and attempt to protect the FBI from executive branch checks on it.

All of this is foolish. It's *good* that the legislative branch checks the executive branch, and it's *good* that the executive branch must remain in control of executive branch agencies. Here's the easy test: How would you feel if the situations were reversed? How would Republicans feel about an emergency declaration from a Democratic president to shift funds to leftist priorities? How would Democrats feel about Republican attempts to seize control of the FBI for purposes of investigating a Democratic president?

Nobody ought to trust institutions enough to grant them unchecked power. And no one ought to trust the people enough to allow us to do so.

Factually Incorrect Cannot Be Morally Correct

January 23, 2019

A few weeks ago, the Fresh Face of the Democratic Party, Rep. Alexandria Ocasio-Cortez, D-N.Y., gave one of the great defenses in the history of politics. Accused of fibbing and twisting facts to meet her radical agenda, Ocasio-Cortez explained, "I think that there's a lot of people more concerned about being precisely, factually and semantically correct than about being morally right." Her statement was widely derided. But it is indeed the mantra of today's politics. The narrative must be preserved at all costs—even the cost of the truth.

Take, for example, Ocasio-Cortez's ridiculous statements this week on the state of modern America. She explained that her plan to radically restructure the American economy is necessitated by the fact that "the world is gonna end in 12 years if we don't address climate change." She added: "And your biggest issue is how are we gonna pay for it? And like, this is the war—this is our World War II." Now, put aside her Nostradamus-like assertion regarding the incoming apocalypse. The important part followed: "How are we saying, 'Take it easy,' when the America that we're living in today is so dystopian with people sleeping in their cars so they can work a second job without health care and we're told to settle down."

Now, when President Trump describes America as a dystopia rife with crime and suffering, the media point out that America is hardly a hellhole—we're the most prosperous country in the history of the world. But when the charming AOC uses her false depiction of America to press for higher marginal tax rates, we're supposed to buy her story.

This gap between the facts and the narrative dominates our politics. Here's how the narrative chain works: Somebody makes a fact-free accusation of X, which supports the more general narrative, Y, supported by the political left or right. Opponents debunk X. That attempt to debunk X is taken as evidence that opponents don't take the problem of Y seriously enough. Facts are marshaled to show that Y is true, even if X isn't. In a peculiar way, the lack of facts to back X lends passion to those who defend Y—it allows them to malign the motives of those who don't defend Y.

Let's take an example. The students of Covington Catholic High School are accused of mobbing and mocking a Native American veteran. This incident supports the broader narrative that Trump supporters, religious Americans and young white men are emissaries of racism and toxic masculinity. Then it turns out that the video has been taken wildly out of context and deliberately misinterpreted. Many advocates of the narrative immediately declare that while this incident is a poor example, the overall narrative is true—and that leaping to conclusions will be justified next time, in order to prove that the overall narrative ought to be taken seriously. The only price: whomever is next maligned without facts.

This pattern will continue to dominate our politics so long as we ascribe malign motives to those who wait for the facts to emerge—and so long as we reward those who jump to conclusions in taking Y seriously. Waiting must become the order of the day. If it doesn't, politics is going to get a lot worse, and quickly,

The Democrats' Radicalism Problem

January 30, 2019

President Trump is deeply unpopular. According to RealClearPolitics, his favorability ratings now stand at just 41 percent—near-historic lows. This means that Democrats have the upper hand heading into 2020. All they have to do is *not* be radically insane.

And they just can't do it.

Sen. Kamala Harris, D-Calif., the media darling of the moment, stated on a CNN town hall this week that she wants to fully abolish private health insurance, ban all semi-automatic weapons and rid the American economy of carbon emissions within a decade.

None of these positions are popular. Americans are interested in the idea of Medicare-for-All so long as there are no costs. The minute they're told that there may be delays in receiving care, as there are in nearly all countries with socialized medicine, support plummets to just 26 percent, according to a Kaiser Family Foundation poll. Only 37 percent support Medicare-for-All if it means merely raising taxes. How about banning all semi-automatic weapons? As of October, 57 percent of Americans opposed banning semi-automatics. And when it comes to abolishing private cars—which would essentially be necessary to achieve the goals of the so-called Green New Deal—that proposal wouldn't even chart.

Yet the Democratic primaries will require nearly every Democrat to embrace each of these positions. That's probably why Democrats are quaking in their boots at the possibility of a third-party run by former Starbucks CEO Howard Schultz. Schultz has declared nationalized health care an impossibility; he has talked about the dangers of our massive national debt; he has opposed a 70 percent income tax rate. "I respect the Democratic Party," Schultz told CNBC this week. "I no longer feel affiliated because I don't know their views represent the majority of Americans."

Now, Schultz may be a boring billionaire, but at least he isn't pushing proposals so loony they alienate vast swaths of the American public. Democrats want to have it both ways: They want to push radical leftist policy, but they don't want the blowback such policies entail. They want to pretend that radical leftism is popular even as they implicitly acknowledge the fact that it's not all that popular.

Hence New York Times columnist Michelle Goldberg's fulminating over Schultz's candidacy. She writes, "this frustrated executive's politics aren't widely shared by people who haven't been to Davos." Trump's riding in the low 40s. Democrats shouldn't have to sweat out fringe candidacies. Yet that's what they're doing, because they know they've pushed too far to the left.

There's an easy answer to the Schultz conundrum for Democrats: Stop embracing the radical id of your own base. But that would involve recognizing that Trump's unpopularity isn't equivalent to support for radicalism. And Democrats will never acknowledge it—not as long as the hope remains that Trump's unpopularity will translate into extreme leftist policy, the likes of which the republic has rarely seen.

Baby Killing Is Fine. Yearbook Photos Are the Problem

February 6, 2019

Last week, Virginia Gov. Ralph Northam was hit with a shocking blast from the past: a photo on his medical school yearbook page of a man in blackface and another man in a Ku Klux Klan outfit. Northam quickly apologized for the photo, then said he wasn't in the photo and then admitted he had once worn blackface and dressed up as Michael Jackson for a dance contest. He nearly moonwalked at a press conference before his wife gave him a look that could curdle milk.

For this sin—the sin of an old, disgusting, racially insensitive photo—Northam now finds his political career on the skids. As of this writing, he's hanging on by his fingernails, even as his lieutenant governor struggles with dicey sexual assault allegations.

The same week that Northam found himself in hot water, he endorsed a Virginia bill that would have broadened the ability of women to obtain an abortion up to the point of birth. Virginia Delegate Kathy Tran, a sponsor of the bill, stated in defense of her legislation that women would be able to obtain an abortion during *labor*. Northam then defended the bill, adding that if a baby were born alive during such an abortion—he assumed that the abortion would be due to "severe deformities" or "a fetus that's not viable"—then the baby could be "kept comfortable" while the family and the doctor decide its fate.

Even in the least appalling reading of his comments, Northam clearly endorsed infanticide. The only question is whether he endorsed the murder of fully born children.

Yet these comments did not merit his ouster. In fact, they didn't even merit an argument inside the Democratic Party about the extremism of the pro-choice position. Last month, Democrats in the state of New York cheered wildly for a law that opened the floodgates to third-trimester abortion, with Gov. Andrew Cuomo ordering state sites to be illuminated in pink in celebration of the potential murder of the unborn. The Democratic governor of Rhode Island endorsed a similar bill; Democrats in Vermont attempted to pass an even more extreme bill that would enshrine abortion as a "fundamental right" for the entirety of the pregnancy period.

All of this is apparently less controversial than a three-decades-old photograph showing a medical student in blackface. Endorsing the killing of babies during dilation *today*—not 30 years ago, not 30 weeks ago—is considered less of a faux pas than racially offensive idiocy during the Reagan presidency.

The morality of our nation may be skewed beyond repair. Northam certainly deserves criticism for his yearbook stupidities, and for his even more idiotic response. But if the American people are more consumed with the consequences of insulting costumes from 1984 than the murder of the unborn today, we deserve everything we have coming to us.

The Republican Pouncing Problem

February 13, 2019

In the past few weeks, prominent Democrats have endorsed infanticide; admitted to dressing in blackface; called for an end to fossil fuels, airplanes and farting cows; and trafficked in open anti-Semitism. None of this is a serious problem for many in the media. For members of the media, the *real* story is that Republicans keep pouncing.

Two weeks ago, Virginia Gov. Ralph Northam stated in an interview that he favors legislation that would allow a woman to abort a baby at the point of dilation and then added that in certain cases in which a baby would be born alive, the baby would be kept "comfortable" while parents and doctors decide what to do with it. This seems rather radical. Here was the Washington Post's take, as said in a headline: "Republicans seize on liberal positions to paint Democrats as radical." The positions, you see, are ackshually mainstream. It's just that Republicans *seized* on them and *painted* them as radical.

Last week, Rep. Alexandria Ocasio-Cortez, D-N.Y., released a Green New Deal backgrounder and FAQ on her website—and her staff sent the six-page document to a variety of media outlets. The document happens to be fully insane. It calls for America to be carbon emissions-free within 10 years without use of nuclear power. It suggests that every building in the country be either replaced or retrofitted. It calls for universal health care, free college education, replacement of airplanes with high-speed trains, replacement of "every combustion-engine vehicle," government-provided jobs, abolition of "farting cows" and, best of all, total "economic security" for anyone "unwilling to work." The proposal is so farcical that even Democrats ran from it screaming. AOC took down it down from her website and then deployed campaign aides to state that the document was "accidentally" released as an "early draft." Unsurprisingly, no revised draft has been posted.

Here is The New York Times' headline: "Ocasio-Cortez Team Flubs a Green New Deal Summary, and Republicans Pounce."

This week, Rep. Ilhan Omar, D-Minn., engaged in open anti-Semitism, suggesting that American support for Israel is "all about the Benjamins" and then doubling down on that comment by blaming the American Israel Public Affairs Committee for America's pro-Zionist attitude. This follows years of overtly anti-Semitic content from Omar, as well as from Rep. Rashida Tlaib, D-Mich., who suggested back in January that Americans who like Israel suffer from dual loyalty and "forgot which country they represent."

Politico tweeted: "The Republican Party has a new trio of Democratic villains: Rashida Tlaib, Ilhan Omar, and Alexandria Ocasio-Cortez."

Now, pouncing is never a story. Ever. It is a simple fact of politics that when people screw up, their political opponents react with alacrity. Highlighting that response rather than the underlying screw-up is the equivalent of a headline that reads "Sun Rises in Morning." Yet that's what the media do ... whenever Democrats screw up. Republican gaffes are a story in and of themselves. Democratic gaffes aren't a story; Republican nastiness is.

All of which demonstrates that a huge swath of the media is inseparable from the Democratic Party. If your first response to Democratic nut-jobbery is to get defensive about Republican blowback, you're no longer a journalist. You're merely a hack. You are, as President Trump would put it, "fake news"—an activist masquerading as a journalist.

I suppose this means I'm pouncing on the media, though.

3 Lessons From the Jussie Smollett Hoax

February 20, 2019

So, Jussie Smollett was lying.

The "Empire" actor claimed that when he was walking home at 2 a.m. in Chicago, in the midst of the polar vortex, he was accosted by two assailants, both of whom shouted anti-gay and anti-black slurs at him. They then attempted to throw a noose around his neck and pour what he thought was bleach on him while shouting, "This is MAGA country!" he says.

None of this is true. Police now believe that Smollett paid two of his friends to stage the entire attack.

Why, exactly, would Smollett do it? He is a successful actor on a hit television show. He's been continuously working in Hollywood for years, with roles in the 2017 films "Marshall" and "Alien: Covenant." He's not exactly a textbook victim.

The answer to this question makes for some uncomfortable lessons.

First, alleged victims sometimes have an incentive to lie. For several years, each time an alleged victim tells an unverified and unverifiable story, we are told that we must believe that victim's story. Why? Because why would the victim lie? But this is often untrue. Smollett had an incentive to lie: unending media attention, fawning sycophancy from politicians and the potential for even greater Hollywood stardom. If Smollett had gotten away with his hoax, he'd be the face of gay, black suffering in the United States. Few had heard of Smollett before this story. Suddenly, he found himself on "Good Morning America," telling the world about his own bravery. That's a lucrative career path.

Second, hoaxers can read the tea leaves. There's a reason that the most prominent racial and sexual hoaxes have generally flattered the political sensibilities of the political left. Right-wing hoaxes might catch the attention of right-wing sources, but left-wing sources are far more powerful and plentiful. Imagine if a MAGA-hatted young Republican had accused two young black men of assaulting him while shouting, "F--- Trump!" That story might get play on talk radio and Fox News, but it wouldn't earn one iota of attention from celebrity culture or the mainstream media.

Third, social media makes hoaxes infinitely easier. There are large-scale incentives for jumping on every story before the facts are clear, which is why both Sens. Cory Booker, D-N.J., and Kamala Harris, D-Calif., both running for president, tweeted their support for Smollett ... and then had to backtrack radically, suggesting as the hoax emerged that they had to wait for more facts. Being the first to rip America bears political fruit; waiting for the whole story often earns public castigation for insufficient sensitivity.

All of this means that the hoaxes won't stop anytime soon. The incentives simply aren't aligned for hoaxes to end. Media members are too eager to buy into stories that support their preferred narratives; social media is too eager to engage in pile-ons of epic proportions; hoaxes are obviously eager to make a buck or win some fame. Which means that we should all wait next time we hear a story too good to be true.

But we won't. Nobody knows who the next Jussie Smollett will be. But within a few weeks, we'll surely know.

Venezuela and the Myth of Kinder, Gentler Socialism

February 27, 2019

Venezuela is a socialist country. Venezuela is also a dictatorship. Currently, Venezuela has fallen into open violence and complete chaos, with the strongman Nicolas Maduro ordering troops to open fire on those attempting to bring humanitarian aid into the country.

Yet, strangely, Maduro still has his defenders. Sen. Bernie Sanders, I-Vt., the leading declared Democratic 2020 presidential candidate and avowed socialist, refuses to label Maduro a "dictator." Sen. Chris Murphy, D-Conn., said in full 9/11 truther mode, "Democrats need to be careful about a potential trap being set by Trump et al in Venezuela. Cheering humanitarian convoys sounds like the right thing to do, but what if it's not about the aid?" Fresh Face of the Democratic Party Rep. Alexandria Ocasio-Cortez, D-N.Y., has remained shockingly silent about Venezuela, except to tell The Daily Caller News Foundation, "I think that, you know, the humanitarian crisis is extremely concerning but, you know, when we use non-Democratic means to determine leadership, that's also concerning, as well." Rep. Ilhan Omar, D-Minn., another Fresh Face of the Democratic Party, grilled U.S. envoy to Venezuela Elliott Abrams in an obvious attempt to stall on behalf of a gentler approach to Maduro.

Why the shocking unwillingness by the socialist hard-liners in the Democratic Party to condemn Maduro and join the rest of the world in calling for his ouster? After all, we've been assured by Sanders, AOC, Omar and others that *true* socialism isn't at stake in Venezuela—*true* socialism can be found in nations like Sweden, Norway and Denmark. Yet even so, these socialist Democrats can't find it in their hearts to cut ties with Venezuela.

How strange.

Perhaps it's because Sanders and his crowd understand full well that Venezuela is an excellent case study in socialism—nationalization of major industries by a centralized government, abolition of the profit motive and redistribution of resources via tyranny. After all, it wasn't that long ago that Sanders was praising the Soviet Union (he said it had "a whole variety of programs for young people and cultural programs which go far beyond what we do in this country"), Nicaraguan Sandanista Daniel Ortega and Cuba's Fidel Castro ("... he educated their kids, gave their kids health care, totally transformed the society.").

And then there's the inconvenient fact that the countries that Sanders himself calls socialist totally reject the label. Former Swedish Prime Minister Carl Bildt launched into Sanders this week, stating, "Bernie Sanders was lucky to be able to get to the Soviet Union in 1988 and praise all its stunning socialist achievements before the entire system and empire collapsed under the weight of its own spectacular failures." In 2015, Danish Prime Minister Lars Rasmussen scoffed at Sanders' dreams of a socialist utopia, noting, "The Nordic model is an expanded welfare state which provides a high level of security to its citizens, but it is also a successful market economy with much freedom to pursue your dreams and life your life as you wish."

Here is the sad truth about socialism: Socialism drives economies into the ground in exact proportion to its prominence in the economy. Capitalism creates prosperity. It's convenient for Sanders and company to point to the Nordic countries as models of socialism when they are obviously founded on free markets, with socialistic redistribution schemes stacked atop that free market foundation. But deep down, Sanders knows that the truer reflection of socialism lies in Venezuela, Cuba and the Soviet Union. And that's why Sanders simply can't bring himself to disown Venezuelan socialism, even to prop up the lie that socialism wasn't truly tried in Venezuela.

The Righteous Mission of Bernie Sanders

March 6, 2019

Sen. Bernie Sanders' perspective on the world is deeply wrong. He has spent his career defending oppressive socialist regimes across the planet while criticizing the supposed predation of the United States; he has generated no legislation of significance in decades of public service. His platform currently advocates for tax rates that mirror those of the Nordic countries, spending tens of trillions of dollars on various government-provided entitlements, and the destruction of well over 150 million people's private health insurance plans.

But there is one area in which Bernie Sanders represents the better angels of the Democratic nature: race.

Sanders is currently being excoriated by a radical segment of the Democratic Party for his racial views. Despite the fact that Sanders marched with Martin Luther King Jr. during the civil rights movement, he is now viewed as retrograde in his racial viewpoints. That's because he believes that socialism is a cure-all for racial discrimination. For example, Sanders refuses to endorse racial reparations, stating instead that broad-based governmental programs ought to benefit those who are lowest on the income ladder. He has likewise stated that candidates ought to be judged based on their ideas rather than their intersectional characteristics. In 2016, Sanders stated, "One of the struggles that you're going to be seeing in the Democratic Party is whether we go beyond identity politics."

Sanders, in other words, separates people by class rather than race. That's wrong, too: In America, we're all individuals who move between classes with remarkable rapidity. We are not the 1 percent and the 99 percent; in fact, a huge number of those in the top 1 percent every year were not in the 1 percent in prior years, and will not be again in future years. We do not have a stable hierarchy of income in the United States. Sanders, by his own statement, grew up in a lower-middle-class household in Brooklyn; he now has two vacation homes despite never having worked a serious job.

But if we're going to talk about damaging divisions in America, class divisions take a back seat to racial divisions. That's because America doesn't actually have a real history of class divisions—we've been an overwhelmingly middle-class country for centuries, as Alexis de Tocqueville noted. But our racial divisions have been all too real, marking the greatest blot on America's history.

Proponents of intersectional politics point this out, suggesting that those racial divisions continue to dominate American life. But that's simply not true. In reality, America is less racist now than it ever has been; laws that discriminate on the basis of race are unconstitutional; racial politics has been relegated, for the most part, to mind reading the supposed motives of political opponents. Sanders implicitly acknowledges that truth when he calls for solutions that do not take into account race as a key factor.

And for that sin, Sanders is being othered by many in the Democratic Party. He's viewed as old-fashioned, hopeful, naive—Trumplike in his view of race, a proponent of a hackneyed baby-boomer "Green Book" mentality. He's outdated and wrong.

Thus Sanders must be ousted for his failure to conform to the intersectional politics that now dominate the Democratic Party. But here's the thing: At least when it comes to his implicit treatment of race, Sanders is closer to the truth than his Democratic opponents. And if Democrats don't recognize this, they'll be abandoning the possibility of a broad-based coalition that crosses racial lines in favor of a racially polarized one that exacerbates them.

Government Isn't the Social Fabric

March 13, 2019

Over the weekend, Democratic Fresh Face and socialist darling Rep. Alexandria Ocasio-Cortez, D-N.Y., spoke at the South by Southwest conference. While sitting amidst the enormous bounty provided by capitalism—top-notch electronic equipment, a massive crowd of paid ticket holders—AOC tore into capitalism. She called the system that has raised 80 percent of the globe from extreme poverty since 1980 "irredeemable." She railed against the injustice of people having to work jobs rather than write poetry—as though socialist countries are famous for ensuring that people work only the jobs they find spiritually rewarding.

Finally, she settled on her most damning line of attack: America as it currently stands is "garbage," because in the United States, "if you don't have a job, you are left to die."

That's an odd critique given the long history of death associated with socialism—some 45 million deaths under Mao, some 30 to 40 million under Stalin and some 2 million under Pol Pot, for starters. But it's an even odder critique given the fact that life expectancy has radically increased under capitalism: In 1850, the average European life expectancy was 36.3 years, while today, the average life expectancy across Europe stands at approximately 80. Furthermore, the United States currently boasts effective full employment. Our poor are in danger of dying of *obesity*, not starvation. And we spend, on a state and federal level, at least $1.1 trillion per year on means-tested welfare programs. By census data, that amounts to nearly

$9,000 per household in the United States annually, or nearly $28,000 for every person living in poverty in the United States.

But let's take Ocasio-Cortez's argument to the logical extreme. Presumably, she's in favor of these expensive government programs and thinks that in their absence, the poor would be left to die in the United States. Is that true?

Absolutely not. Ocasio-Cortez makes the same mistake so many on the left do: She conflates government redistributionism with the social fabric itself. In her view, there is no social fabric absent government. What's more, nongovernmental social fabric is a *threat* to equality—as Sen. Bernie Sanders, I-Vt., put it in 1981, "I don't believe in charities." The New York Times reported that Sanders questioned the "fundamental concepts on which charities are based," since government was the only entity positioned to help the impoverished.

That's sheer nonsense. Before the rise of the massive welfare state, Americans gave massive amounts of charity. In 1926, religious congregations spent more than $150 million on projects other than church maintenance and upkeep, with state governments spending just $23 million and local governments spending $37 million, according to economists Jonathan Gruber of MIT and Daniel Hungerman of the University of Notre Dame. Americans have always given enormous sums to charity. And those charitable activities come along with something government redistributionism can't achieve: a feeling of social belonging and of membership in a social fabric.

Free markets create prosperity. And government isn't the social fabric. Recognition of those two simple facts explains what made America thrive—and can help us thrive again, in spite of those who would prefer to tear down markets and social fabric and replace them with the heavy hand of centralized government.

How to Silence Debate, New Zealand Edition

March 20, 2019

Rep. Ilhan Omar, D-Minn., has unleashed a barrage of openly anti-Semitic commentary. She suggested that Israel had "hypnotized the world." She recently suggested that Jewish money lay behind American support for Israel. Finally, she suggested that American Israel supporters are representatives of dual loyalty. Her fellow Democrats shielded her from blowback by subsuming a resolution that condemns her anti-Semitism within a broader resolution that condemns intolerance of all types. Many of them suggested that labeling Omar's anti-Semitism actually represents a type of censorship—an attempt to quash debate about Israel, though none of Omar's comments even critiqued the Israeli government, and though many on the left have made anti-Israel arguments without invoking anti-Semitism.

Now Omar's defenders have come out of the woodwork to suggest that criticism of her anti-Semitism was somehow responsible for the white supremacist shooting of 50 innocent people in a mosque in Christchurch, New Zealand. Two protesters, New York University students and best friends Leen Dweik and Rose Asaf, confronted Chelsea Clinton, who had gently chided Omar for her Jew hatred. "After all that you have done, all the Islamophobia that you have stoked," Dweik screamed, "this, right here, is the result of a massacre stoked by people like you and the words you put out in the world. ... Forty-nine people died because of the rhetoric you put out there." Dweik, it should be noted, has called for the complete elimination of Israel.

Her message was parroted by terror supporter Linda Sarsour, who tweeted: "I am triggered by those who piled on Representative Ilhan Omar and incited a hate mob against her until she got assassination threats now giving condolences to our community. What we need you to do is reflect on how you contribute to islamophobia and stop doing that."

Meanwhile, mainstream commentators attempted to use the New Zealand anti-Muslim terror attack to blame critics of radical Islam. Omer Aziz, writing for The New York Times, slammed Jordan Peterson for calling Islamophobia "a word created by fascists" and Sam Harris for calling it "intellectual blood libel." Bill Maher has come in for similar criticism; so have I, mostly for a video I cut in 2014 in which I read off poll statistics from various Muslim countries on a variety of topics, concluding that a huge percentage of Muslims believed radical things.

Here's the truth: Radical Islam is dangerous. The Islamic world has a serious problem with radical Islam. And large swaths of the Muslim world are, in fact, hostile to Western views on matters ranging from freedom of speech to women's rights. To conflate that obvious truth with the desire to murder innocents in Christchurch is intellectual dishonesty of the highest sort. If we want more Muslims living in liberty and freedom, we must certainly demolish white supremacism—and we must also demolish radical Islam, devotees of which were responsible for an estimated 84,000 deaths in 2017 alone, most of those victims Muslim.

And here's another truth: Anti-Semitism is ugly, whether it's coming from white supremacists or Ilhan Omar. Making that point has nothing to do with the killing of Muslims in Christchurch.

So long as the media continue to push the narrative that criticism of Islam is tantamount to incitement of murder, radical Islam will continue to flourish. So long as the media continue to cover for the dishonest argument that criticism of anti-Semitism forwards the goals of white supremacists, anti-Semitism will continue to flourish. Honest discussion about hard issues isn't incitement.

Why We Don't Trust Our Institutions?

March 27, 2019

This week, special counsel Robert Mueller released his long-awaited report on alleged collusion between the Trump campaign and the Russian government to impact the 2016 election. His conclusion: no collusion. It's been apparent for quite some time that Mueller would end up here—every indictment has been based on an ancillary crime, not the chief question of election conspiracy. Nonetheless, the final result came as a bombshell.

That's because for two years, the mainstream media have treated Trump-Russian collusion as a reality. Facts would eventually arrive to fill in the gaps in the narrative. Surely, Trump's presidency would crumble when the deus ex machina, the Mueller report, arrived.

But that didn't happen. And so the media are left with unending egg on their faces, having suggested continuously for years that Trump was illegitimately elected, and that his campaign had engaged in treasonous activity to prevent the rightful president, Hillary Clinton, from assuming office.

That narrative found support in leaders from the Democratic intelligence community. Rep. Adam Schiff, D-Calif., of the House Intelligence Committee spent years camping outside CNN headquarters in a pup tent, ready at a moment's notice to suggest access to secret information that would certainly take down the president. Former CIA Director John Brennan accused Trump of treason, standing on his resume to do so. Former Director of National Intelligence James Clapper stated that Watergate "pales" beside allegations of coordination between the Trump campaign and Russia. Former acting FBI Director Andrew McCabe suggested that Trump could be a Russian cat's paw. Former FBI Director James Comey implied that Trump had fired him for nefarious reasons, not because Trump was angry with Comey for failing to announce that Trump wasn't under investigation.

Our intelligence leadership, in other words, humiliated themselves.

Meanwhile, in Chicago, Cook County prosecutors agreed to drop charges against alleged hate crime hoaxer Jussie Smollett, who alleged that he was beaten by two white men in the middle of the night on the streets of Chicago. Chicago Mayor Rahm Emanuel called the dropped charges a "whitewash." Chicago Police Superintendent Eddie Johnson bashed Smollett's defense team, explaining, "they chose to hide behind secrecy and broker a deal to circumvent the judicial system."

Why have key institutions betrayed their initial mission? Mission creep. The job of the media is to objectively cover stories, not to drive narratives. The job of the intelligence community is to diligently follow evidence, not to follow its cognitive bias. The job of the state's attorney is to prosecute crime, not to play politics.

Without defined roles, our institutions crumble. Treating institutions as mere tools to be wielded in pursuit of some higher goal leads to the destruction of those institutions; they become little more than weapons, aimed by those in power. That's dangerous stuff. We should be able to trust our press. If we can't, then we can no longer base our republican decision-making on a common set of facts. We should be able to trust our intelligence community and our prosecutors. If we can't, then we can't support granting them the power they require to protect us.

But protecting institutions has taken a back seat to do-goodism. "Objective" journalists see themselves as crusaders; political members of the intelligence community see themselves as protectors; prosecutors see themselves as emissaries of social justice rather than as part of a broader, more objective system of determining guilt and innocence. Institutions only mean more than the people who comprise them when the people who comprise them value the institutions more than their own politics. That's being lost. The result is the continued atomization of our society.

When You Don't Appreciate Your Civilization

April 3, 2019

Last week, former Vice President Joe Biden spoke at the Biden Courage Awards ceremony in preparation for his presidential campaign launch. There, in an attempt to forestall claims that as a white man, he simply isn't intersectional enough to compete in the Democratic primaries, he critiqued a central pillar of Western civilization as inherently racist. "Back in the late 1300s, so many women were dying at the hands of their husbands because they were chattel, just like the cattle, or the sheep, that the court of common law decided they had to do something about the extent of the deaths," Biden fibbed. "So you know what they said? No man has a right to chastise his woman with a rod thicker than the circumference of his thumb. This is English jurisprudential culture, a white man's culture. It's got to change. It's got to change."

Biden's take was, as always, historically illiterate. The "rule of thumb" story has been circulating for years—and it has been repeatedly debunked. There was no "rule of thumb," as feminist scholar Christina Hoff Sommers points out. "On the contrary," she writes, "British law since the 1700s and our American laws predating the Revolution prohibit wife beating." In actuality, the phrase originated in craftsmen so expert that they could perform tasks without precise measuring tools.

More importantly, however, Biden's characterization of "English jurisprudential culture" as "white man's culture" is profoundly disturbing. English jurisprudential culture is rooted in the belief in the rule of law, due process of law, equal rights under law; English jurisprudential culture is responsible for preserving the natural rights we hold dear, rights which were imperfectly but increasingly extended over time to more and more human beings, particularly minorities. No less a leftist figure than Barack Obama explained just that in 2009, saying he sought a system at Guantanamo Bay that "adheres to the rule of law, habeas corpus, basic principles of Anglo-American legal system."

Protection of individual rights—and in particular, minority rights—lies at the heart of English jurisprudence. Yet Biden boiled down those rights to racial privilege. And the attempt to reduce the fundamental principles of our civilization to a mask for racial hierarchical power is both false and frightening. It suggests that those principles ought to be undermined for purposes of disestablishing that supposed hierarchy. Get rid of English jurisprudential law, presumably, in order to fight racism.

Ironically, reduction of Western civilization to racial supremacy isn't just a strategy of the intersectional left; it's a strategy of the despicable alt-right, which champions Western civilization as white civilization and then seeks to rip away the universalism of its principles from nonwhite people. Thus, the very term "Western civilization" is under assault by a variety of political forces seeking to tear out eternal truths and natural rights in the name of tribalism.

But that's not what Western civilization is about at all. Western civilization was built on Judeo-Christian values and Greek reason, culminating in a perspective on natural rights that is preserved by institutions like English jurisprudence. It is thanks to those philosophical principles that free markets, free speech and free association have grown and flourished. Only if we re-enshrine those principles, rather than undermine them, will our prosperity and freedoms be preserved.

The Open Borders Agenda Rears Its Ugly Head

April 10, 2019

This week, President Trump fired his homeland security secretary, Kirstjen Nielsen. Nielsen was, according to media and the Democrats, a monster of the highest order. She was allegedly the force behind the caging of children (that practice began under President Barack Obama and actually ended under President Trump); she was supposedly a barbarian focused on keeping innocent brown children out of America.

And Trump dumped her because even she was not cruel enough to please Genghis Trump, the left claimed. Stephen Colbert joked, "Sure, she put kids in cages, but Trump was upset. ... So he just needs someone who can be crueler to children than Kirstjen Nielsen." Jimmy Kimmel made nearly the same joke: "Goodbye, Kirstjen, and whoever replaces you permanently is going to have some very big cages to fill." Trevor Noah quipped, "Basically, the only job she can get now is working with R. Kelly."

In reality, Trump fired Nielsen because he believed she hadn't properly taken measures to rein in the humanitarian crisis at the border. That was half true—she didn't react with alacrity to change the necessary Homeland Security regulations, for example. But it was also a result of Trump's changing whims with regard to border strategy. Trump was in favor of a no-tolerance border policy that necessarily resulted in family separations; then he was against it; then he was for it; then he was against it.

Most of that vacillation resulted not from brutal bigotry, however, but from a simple fact: Democrats have simply not provided Border Patrol and Immigration and Customs Enforcement with the resources necessary to properly control the border. Federal courts have ruled that families cannot be held together in custody for longer than 20 days; children must be released to guardians outside detention. This means that the Trump administration, like the Obama administration before it, was left with a choice: Either release parents along with children, or separate parents from children.

The federal courts have made the situation even less tenable. They have stated that the Trump administration cannot work with the Mexican government to house potential asylum claimants on the Mexican side of the border to keep families together; they have stated that the Trump administration cannot separate families for prolonged periods of time. A series of conflicting lower-court rulings has left the general policy in limbo.

This means that Congress ought to act. Everyone should be on the same page with regard to those crossing the border illegally. We should have an expedient system for determining the validity of asylum claims; we should give families the option of staying together in detention pending such determination.

But Democrats in Congress refuse to act. They won't change the regulations to allow families to remain together in custody, and they won't provide the funding necessary to keep detained families in some level of comfort. Instead, they snipe at the supposed cruelty of the Trump administration, which simply seeks to end the policy of "catch and release" that results in hundreds of thousands of illegal immigrants remaining indefinitely in the country.

This week, Tom Perez, chairman of the Democratic National Committee, revealed the truth about the Democratic agenda: It's not about compassion at all, but about politics. "Tough doesn't equal smart," Perez stated. "Tough equals dumb." The only truly dumb thing is continuing to play politics with the lives of people crossing the border illegally and American citizens being forced to cope with the price of illegal immigration.

Criticism of Ilhan Omar Isn't Incitement

April 17, 2019

A couple of years ago, I spoke at the University of California, Berkeley. My presence was apparently so offensive to a particular group of people that hundreds of police officers were necessary to ensure the safety of the event. As I spoke inside, the protesters milled about, chanting and shouting. One of their favorite ditties: "SPEECH IS VIOLENCE!"

This, of course, is patent nonsense. Speech is not violence—and violence is not speech. Equating the two is the hallmark of a tyrannical worldview: If I can treat your speech as violence, then I am justified in using violence to suppress your speech. And yet that obvious fallacy has become the rallying cry in defense of execrable Rep. Ilhan Omar, D-Minn.

Omar, who has been content to spout openly anti-Semitic nonsense every several weeks since her election, came under fire this week for her remarks at an event in late March, shortly after her Democratic colleagues covered for her Jew hatred by watering down a resolution of condemnation. Speaking before the historically Hamas-friendly Council on American-Islamic Relations (CAIR), Omar unleashed a barrage of lies about the maltreatment of Muslims throughout America. In the midst of that barrage, she dropped a line about Sept. 11: "CAIR was founded after 9/11 because they recognized that some people did something and that all of us were starting to lose access to our civil liberties."

That minimization of 9/11—and that's what it is—resulted in blowback from conservatives. It's not as though Omar's history of treating terrorism with kid gloves is anything new, after all. In 2013, Omar did an interview in which she chided one of her professors for treating terrorist groups with horror while failing to do the same to America, England and the military: "The thing that was interesting in the class was every time the professor said 'Al Qaida,' his shoulders went up. ... But you know, it is that you don't say 'America' with an intensity. You don't say 'England' with the intensity. You don't say 'the Army' with the intensity."

In 2016, Omar wrote a letter to a judge asking for lighter sentences for men accused of being Islamic State group recruits, noting that these men merely "chose violence to combat direct marginalization" and calling their recruitment "a consequential mistake" that resulted from "systematic alienation."

In 2017, Omar wrote for Time magazine: "We must confront that our nation was founded by the genocide of indigenous people and on the backs of slaves, that we maintain global power with the tenor of neocolonialism. ... Our national avoidance tactic has been to shift the focus to potential international terrorism." That's not exactly a ringing rebuke of international terrorism.

But now Omar is criticizing those who merely quote her as inciting violence. She has claimed that President Trump, who posted a video that juxtaposed footage of 9/11 with her "some people did something" comment, is responsible for an uptick in the number of death threats she has received. Her close friend Rep. Alexandria Ocasio-Cortez, D-N.Y., went so far as to compare Omar to a victim of the Holocaust.

This is immoral in the extreme. Omar isn't a victim because she's being criticized. And speech isn't incitement. Sen. Bernie Sanders wasn't responsible for the congressional baseball game shooting. Former President Barack Obama wasn't responsible for the Dallas police shooting. And Trump isn't responsible for those who send Omar death threats. He's responsible for criticizing her—rightly, in this case. Democrats who hide behind the charge of incitement are simply attempting to quash debate. And that's far more dangerous for the future of America than criticizing a radical politician.

Can Joe Biden Apologize His Way to the Presidency?

May 1, 2019

Former vice president and new 2020 Democratic frontrunner Joe Biden has a problem. His problem is simple: He has a record. That record is long and checkered. And that means that Biden has spent the first months of his undeclared campaign apologizing.

In January, Biden apologized for having supported criminal sentencing laws that helped drive down crime in the United States. He did so because those laws are now considered both passe and un-woke—they've been maligned as inherently racist. Thus, Biden stated: "I haven't always been right. I know we haven't always gotten things right, but I've always tried," adding that the bill in the early 1990s "trapped an entire generation" and "was a big mistake when it was made." That's a change from 2016, when Biden told CNBC he wasn't ashamed "at all" for supporting the bill and bragged, "I drafted the bill."

Weeks ago, as Biden prepped his presidential run, he approached Anita Hill, the woman who accused Justice Clarence Thomas of sexual harassment. Hill's testimony was riddled with inconsistencies and outright lies. Biden recognized that at the time—according to former Sen. Arlen Specter's autobiography, Biden told him in 1998 that, with regard to Hill's protestations of memory lapses, "It was clear to me from the way she was answering the questions, she was lying." Now, however, Biden told Hill, "I'm sorry for what happened to you." Hill, for her part, is having none of it—she called his apology insufficient and stated that he owes Americans a more generalized apology.

Then, just four weeks ago, Biden issued a quasi-apology for his habitual invasion of women's personal space. In a two-minute video, he explained: "The boundaries of protecting personal space have been reset. I get it. I get it. I hear what they're saying. I understand. And I'll be much more mindful."

All of this has prompted Damon Linker of The Week to forecast: "Biden will apologize. And then apologize again. And then again. Endlessly. Gracelessly. Until he finally gives up and goes home."

Amazingly, though, all of the things for which Biden is apologizing are things for which he *should not be apologizing*. The early 1990s saw a spike in crime that largely affected minority communities; Hill was probably prevaricating; Biden's invasion of personal space is awkward, but it was never harassment. But in our new political world, running means having to say you're sorry for having a record at all. That's why it was easier for Barack Obama to run than Hillary Clinton—and, in many ways, it was easier for Donald Trump to run than Sen. Ted Cruz. Having a record is a burden.

The power of positive thinking trumps years of experience. After all, you don't have to worry about what Mayor Pete Buttigieg has done since he's never done anything. But you *do* have to worry about Joe Biden's record being rehashed. That's why Biden's best weeks may be his first weeks. As his record reemerges, as other Democrats dig into his past for dirt, Biden will have to get used to saying he's sorry and then hope that Democratic voters choose to take him back.

Why Scorn Matters

May 8, 2019

This week, the Met Gala took place in New York City. The event has always been a showpiece for celebrities seeking to make a splash, from Rihanna in her Pope costume to Katy Perry dressed as a chandelier. This year's event was designed in homage to Susan Sontag's 1964 essay, "Notes on Camp." According to Sontag, "camp" is the "love of the unnatural: of artifice and exaggeration."

In reality, camp according to Sontag is something else: a deliberate attempt to tear down boundaries. "Camp taste," Sontag wrote, "turns its back on the good-bad axis of ordinary aesthetic judgment." "(H)igh culture," Sontag acknowledged, "is basically moral." Camp, by contrast, "is wholly aesthetic." In fact, it "incarnates a victory of 'style' over 'content,' 'aesthetics' over 'morality,' of irony over tragedy." It represents the "solvent of morality" and "neutralizes moral indignation, sponsors playfulness." As Kareem Khubchandani, performance studies and queer studies professor at Tufts University, told NBC News, camp "makes profane the things that are sacred." Sontag said something similar in her essay: Camp is a "sensibility that, among other things, converts the serious into the frivolous."

There is something inherently insulting about camp—particularly camp exhibited to the tunes of hundreds of thousands of dollars by ersatz socialists who consider themselves the moral superiors of those who live in flyover country. Watching celebrities preen on the red carpet while dressed as stripper Mary Poppins (Lady Gaga) or a

Cleopatra knockoff complete with shirtless slaves (Billy Porter) is inherently irritating. There's something sneering and preening about it. But if you're irritated, then you just don't "get it." You don't understand the "irony." You're too sincere, which makes you a bore.

But sincerity builds social fabric; irony tears it down. Measured doses of irony can be helpful in debunking hackneyed ideas, but irony as an entire philosophy is a universal acid. Barack Obama wasn't wrong when he said that Americans should "reject cynicism." The only problem is that he simply labeled all those who opposed his political agenda as cynics.

In reality, cynicism—the mocking, derisive laughter of those who seek to overturn values—can never build anything. Camp doesn't build beauty; it tears it down, drags it through the dust and then laughs. Sontag knew that, which is why she spent most of her career tearing down, not building up. It's not a coincidence that the same person who promoted camp as a way of life also denigrated America—perhaps the most sincere country ever founded, given its reliance on creedal truths rather than mere nationalistic connection—with seething hatred: "If America is the culmination of Western white civilization, as everyone from the Left to the Right declares, then there must be something terribly wrong with Western white civilization. ... The white race is the cancer of human history."

A good deal of America's political polarization right now lies in the belief by those in the middle of the country that elitists on the coasts mock them, deride their pretensions at building as something passe. And those in the middle of the country aren't wrong. Those on the coasts who spend their evenings laughing at the nasty jokes of Stephen Colbert, tut-tutting at the "deplorables" and giddily tweeting over the Panem-style fashion at the Met Gala are doing serious cultural damage. And telling fellow Americans to lighten up won't heal those wounds anytime soon.

The Manufactured Constitutional Crisis

May 15, 2019

Over the past several weeks, Democrats have spent their time defending the absurd notion that America is in the midst of a constitutional crisis. What, pray tell, has initiated this crisis? The supposed unwillingness of Attorney General William Barr to turn over to Congress unredacted sections of the Mueller report, plus underlying grand jury materials. Barr, for his part, correctly points out that the Federal Rules of Criminal Procedure bar him from revealing grand jury testimony. That rule was put in place by Congress itself. Nonetheless, Democrats, seeking to manufacture a feeling of Nixonian chaos, have claimed that the Trump administration is now seeking to block the release of a report that Barr *himself* released. The Mueller report is, indeed, public.

Playing politics with our institutional health is a dangerous game. Here's the truth: Our system of checks and balances is working just fine. Our politicians proclaim that the messy friction between the legislative, executive and judicial branches demonstrates that our politics is unworkable. But that friction is a feature of the system, not a bug. As James Madison explained in Federalist No. 51: "the great security against a gradual concentration of the several powers in the same department, consists in giving to those who administer each department the necessary constitutional means and personal motives to resist encroachments of the others. ... Ambition must be made to counteract ambition."

The founders worried greatly that the supremacy of the legislature would make the executive a mere footstool, propping up legislative authority. To that end, they created a unitary executive with control over law enforcement. And they gave a check against the power of the executive to Congress, which has the ability to defund departments or impeach officials.

Democrats know this. They have the power to impeach William Barr. They're choosing not to do so, because they recognize that their complaint is itself corrupt. Democrats have the power to impeach Donald Trump. They're choosing not to do so, because they recognize that their grounds for such activity are weak in the extreme.

Instead, they participate in a cynical game in which they attack the system of checks and balances itself. That's far more dangerous than any action taken by the Trump administration to date. The same Democrats who claim today that they are deeply concerned about the system of checks and balances are proclaiming from the rooftops that they would be happy to shatter the system to facilitate their agenda. We've heard from Sen. Kamala Harris, D-Calif., that as president, she'd simply use executive authority to set gun law. We've heard from a bevy of Democrats that they'd consider packing the Supreme Court, or abolishing the Electoral College. A few leftist commentators have even suggested abolishing the Senate, given its non-popular representation. We've heard from failed Georgia gubernatorial candidate Stacey Abrams, and her Democratic allies, that her failures were the fault of election fraud; we've heard the same about Andrew Gillum in Florida.

And now Democrats say that Barr's adherence to law is somehow violative of the constitutional order. Undermining the constitutional order publicly, supposedly in order to save it, is nothing but cynical partisanship. But here's the good news: The founders designed a durable system to withstand such nonsense. It continues to work, even if Democrats would prefer it collapse.

No, Abortion Isn't a Constitutional Right

May 22, 2019

In the past several weeks, a bevy of states have passed extensive new restrictions on abortion. Alabama has effectively banned abortion from point of conception. Georgia has banned abortion from the time a heartbeat is detected, as have Ohio, Kentucky and Mississippi. Missouri has banned abortion after eight weeks. Other states are on the move as well.

This has prompted paroxysms of rage from the media and the political left—the same folks who celebrated when New York passed a law effectively allowing abortion up until point of birth and who defended Virginia Gov. Ralph Northam's perverse statements about late-term abortion. According to these thinkers, conservatives have encroached on a supposed "right to abortion" inherent in the Constitution.

This, of course, is a lie. There is no "right to abortion" in the Constitution. The founders would have been appalled by such a statement. The Supreme Court's decision in Roe v. Wade (1973) is a legal monstrosity by every available metric: As legal scholar John Hart Ely wrote, Roe "is not constitutional law and gives almost no sense of an obligation to try to be." The court's rationale is specious; the court relied on the ridiculous precedent in Griswold v. Connecticut (1965) that a broad "right to privacy" can be crafted from "penumbras, formed by emanations." Then the court extended that right to privacy to include the killing of a third party, an unborn human life—and overrode state definitions of human life in the process.

How? The court relied on the self-contradictory notion of "substantive due process"—the belief that a law can be ruled unconstitutional under the Fifth and 14th amendments so long as the court doesn't like the substance of the law. That's asinine, obviously. The due process provision of both amendments was designed to ensure that state and federal government could not remove life, liberty or property without a sufficient legal process, *not* to broadly allow courts to strike down state definitions of conduct that justify removal of life, liberty and property. As Justice Clarence Thomas has written, "The Fourteenth Amendment's Due Process Clause is not a 'secret repository of substantive guarantees against "unfairness."'"

Nonetheless, the notion that such a right to abortion is enshrined in America's moral fabric has taken hold among the intelligentsia. Thus, we now experience the odd spectacle of those on the political left declaring that the Constitution enshrines a right to abortion—yet does not include a right to bear arms, a right to freedom of political speech, a right to retain property free of government seizure or a right to practice religion.

For much of the left, then, the term "constitutional right" has simply come to mean "thing I want." And that is incredibly dangerous, given that the power of the judiciary springs not from legislative capacity but from supposed interpretive power. Judges are not supposed to read things into the Constitution but to properly read the Constitution itself. The use of the judiciary as a club has led to a feeling of radical frustration among Americans; it has radically exacerbated our culture gap.

The legislative moves in Alabama and other states will open a much-needed debate about the role of the states, the role of legislatures and the role of government. All of that is good for the country. Those who insist, however, that the Supreme Court act as a mechanism for their political priorities are of far more danger to the country than that debate.

What We Can Learn From the European Union

May 29, 2019

The European Union Parliament elections this week provided a shock to the system for the center-right and center-left coalition in European politics: The big winners were nationalist movements. In France, Marine Le Pen's immigration-restrictionist National Front defeated the party of the current president, Emmanuel Macron. In Italy, Matteo Salvini's similarly anti-immigration League Party won big. Nationalist parties made gains in Poland, Hungary, Sweden and Great Britain. Euroscepticism is on the rise. And it is being met with a similarly fervent movement of the left: Greens and liberals did shockingly well in Germany.

The main driver behind the new polarization: increased power aggregated in Brussels. While the European Union parliament majority remains pro-EU and pro-immigration, polarization has broken out specifically as a result of the EU overstepping its original boundaries. As Daniel Hannan, Conservative MP and Brexit advocate, writes, "The EU, in short, is responding to the euro and migration crises in the way it responds to everything: with deeper integration."

The burgeoning conflict within the EU should provide the United States with an object lesson: When you maximize the power of the federal government at the expense of the states, you maximize the possibility of polarization. And indeed, that's precisely what we've seen.

Take, for example, transgender bathrooms. If ever there were a local issue, that would be one: What business is it of a New Yorker what North Carolinians do to their bathrooms? Yet North Carolina's bathroom laws prompted national boycotts from residents of other states. That's because the leftist mindset in the United States holds that the federal government ought to weigh in on every issue—and in the absence of federal intervention, informal boycotts should be utilized. Or how about abortion? The Constitution has a process for amendment—but barring such amendment, the issue of abortion remains state-defined in nature. Nonetheless, Netflix announced this week that it will consider boycotting Georgia if Georgia's "heartbeat bill" goes into effect; Sen. Cory Booker, D-N.J., among others, has stated that he wants federal legislation to encode Roe v. Wade.

It's not difficult to imagine these mutual recriminations spiraling. As leftists, motivated by the supposed best of intentions, dictate that the federal government radically escalate its intervention into state domains, conservatives will fight back. The founders recognized that a federal government that usurps state powers would result in the breakdown of the system itself. We're beginning to see that prophecy play out in Europe; the possibility of a similar progression in the United States seems more and more likely.

A system of defined powers is the only system likely to preserve the health and happiness of a diverse society. Whether the European Union survives will depend largely on whether the EU takes account of the inherent powers of the countries it represents; whether the United States survives in the long run will depend on whether the federal government continues to encroach on the power of localities and states without regard for the strictures of the Constitution.

Why Celebrity Politics Matters

June 5, 2019

This week, celebrities emerged from their Hollywood cocoon to sound off on abortion law ... in Georgia. If this sounds bizarre, that's because it is: The people of Georgia don't spend an awful lot of time trying to control the policies of New York or California. Yet the greatest and most moral among us—people who read lines for a living and look attractive for magazine covers—now lecture people thousands of miles away on the necessity of late-term abortion.

Netflix led the charge, announcing that it might cease filming in the state of Georgia should the state impose its "heartbeat bill," protecting the lives of the unborn from the sixth week of pregnancy. Netflix is simultaneously filming in Egypt and Jordan, where abortion is heavily restricted.

Disney soon joined the club, stating that it could pull production as well. Reese Witherspoon spoke up on behalf of females everywhere, saying: "Women of Alabama, I will fight for you. Women of Georgia, I will fight for you. Women of Ohio, Kentucky, Missouri and Mississippi, I will fight for you." Never mind that majorities of women in nearly all of these states are pro-life. Witherspoon knows that *true* women support her agenda. Sophie Turner of "Game of Thrones," too, announced that she wouldn't film in Georgia—after filming her role as Sansa Stark in Northern Ireland, where abortion is illegal.

This sort of disdain of our culture's supposed elite for those who disagree politically is helping drive another wedge into our national divide. It's actually promoting a spiral of division that has severe consequences for our national polis.

Here's how it works.

Culture is supposed to be the binding glue for any nation. The United States is ethnically, politically and religiously diverse. Only a few key threads still bind citizens from New York with citizens from Georgia: symbols like the American flag, institutions like the American military and, yes, water cooler conversations over sports, movies, music and television.

The American left has politicized each of these threads, in effect fraying them. The American flag itself has become a symbol of division, as our cultural betters—and the gimlet-eyed marketing firms that power corporations like Nike—decide to glorify protests against the flag. The American military has been politicized, too, with Hollywood portraying soldiers as either victims or villains (aside from a few rarities like "American Sniper"—which, not coincidentally, did enormous in the box office). Our movies and television and music have become politicized, too, with artists deemed "unwoke" if they refuse to speak up on the issues of the day.

Conservatives have responded by first paying outsized attention to cultural figures who *don't* disdain them—see Trump, Donald—and, second, by showing up in droves to vote. If conservatives can't control the culture, they certainly can control their legislators.

Our cultural arbiters, in turn, have reacted to the political victory of their opposition with renewed attempts to merge culture and politics—they've gotten more extreme, louder, more pronounced in their determination to shift the culture to their point of view. Which will, of course, drive more political divisions.

A pluralistic democracy requires three factors to function: a shared cultural space; a shared belief in key ideas, largely embedded in the Constitution; and a shared willingness to leave one another alone. As each component erodes, so, too, does the possibility of a united country.

The Media/Democrat Complex Strikes Big Tech

June 12, 2019

This week, The New York Times ran a massive piece detailing the supposed radicalization of one Caleb Cain. Cain moved from political liberalism toward self-ascribed "tradcon" status from watching YouTube videos. The New York Times charted this nefarious move by following those videos. The suggestion by The Times was simple: If you watch typical conservative content hosted by people like me, you will eventually end up watching material hosted by alt-right figures. The only solution, presumably, would be for YouTube to downgrade material The Times dislikes.

This attitude isn't only springing from The Times. Axios chief technology correspondent Ina Fried grilled Google CEO Sundar Pichai over the weekend, essentially demanding that YouTube do something to marginalize videos Fried dislikes. Vox ran a full-scale propaganda campaign last week to get conservative comedian Steven Crowder kicked off YouTube for the great sin of making offensive jokes about one of Vox's columnists. Taking their cues from Democratic leaders like House Speaker Nancy Pelosi, various media outlets have spent years suggesting that Facebook's unwillingness to censor political materials led to Hillary Clinton's unjustifiable 2016 presidential defeat.

And it's not just targeting big tech companies. The far-left organization Media Matters for America routinely leads boycott attempts against advertisers who deign to sponsor conservative programs—even if those advertisers sponsor a wide variety of political programming. Pseudojournalists from organizations like Vox and Huffington Post spend their days calling advertisers for comment on various controversial statements by right-wing hosts from Tucker Carlson to Laura Ingraham to Sean Hannity. Their goal isn't to follow the news but to generate a wave of advertiser-pullout announcements likely to do damage to those conservative hosts.

Such censoriousness is rarely, if ever, practiced on the political right. YouTube and Facebook and Twitter are never targeted by conservatives over their unwillingness to shut down opposing points of view; they're criticized for their willingness to kowtow to the political left and its demands for speech suppression. Advertisers on left-wing programming can speak freely, secure in the knowledge that conservatives won't be calling them up to rip them for sponsoring shows like Rachel Maddow's.

That's good. That's how it should be. But for members of the political left, it isn't.

There are two reasons for that. The first is obvious: Those on the political left long ago abandoned the traditional liberal notion that those who disagree have a right to speak. Instead, they must be deplatformed and their advertisers punished, lest their nefarious ideas spread and metastasize. "Repressive tolerance," in the parlance of Herbert Marcuse, has become a mainstay of left-wing thinking.

The other reason is far more cynical: Many in the media want a regeneration of the monopolistic media control of the past. They long for the days when everyone consumed mainstream product to the exclusion of alternative sources. It's no coincidence that YouTube and Facebook have been touting their elevation of "authoritative" news in recent years—they're looking to appease a ravenous media eager to tear them down.

The media and Democrats have picked the right target: The lords of Big Tech are eager to please and frightened of blowback. They're political liberals who can be intimidated into censorship while being simultaneously assured that they're making the world a better place.

They aren't. All it would take for this censorious moment to end would be a little backbone: Facebook, YouTube and Twitter announcing that they won't censor people unless those people violate actual First Amendment principles like incitement and libel; advertisers announcing that they won't pull their dollars based on astroturfed pressure tactics. But backbone is in short supply. And the glut of intimidation won't relax anytime soon.

Freedom From Consequences Isn't Freedom

June 27, 2019

On Monday, Sen. Bernie Sanders, I-Vt., desperate to revive his flagging campaign, proposed a far-reaching plan to wipe out all student debt. That plan falls hard on plans by Sen. Elizabeth Warren, D-Mass., his chief far-left rival for the Democratic presidential nomination, to make college "free" moving forward. Sanders' justification for allocating over $1 trillion of taxpayer money to relieving relatively more well-off people from debt freely incurred: True freedom means living free of consequences. Sanders tweeted: "Are you truly free if you graduate hundreds of thousands of dollars in debt? Are you free if you cannot pursue your dream because you don't make enough to cover your student loan payments? We will #CancelStudentDebt because there is no freedom without economic freedom."

This is an Orwellian redefinition of the term "freedom."

Freedom has traditionally meant the ability to make your own decisions—and to live with the consequences of those decisions. I am free to buy a Lamborghini on credit, if Visa will extend me that credit; I am not deprived of freedom when Visa comes calling with a bill. Economic freedom amounts to the ability to make non-compelled decisions in the economic sphere. Sanders' economic plans offer precisely the reverse.

But Sanders' rhetoric here is merely the latest in a long line of such redefinitions from the American left. Franklin Delano Roosevelt suggested that "true individual freedom cannot exist without economic security and independence"—and proceeded to make more Americans dependent on government than ever before in American history. He declared "freedom from want" in January 1941, in the midst of a second Great Depression of his making—the prior year, the unemployment rate in the United States was 14.45 percent. The mere declaration, as it turned out, did not end want. And the redefinition of freedom as government-sponsored dependency did not end in prosperity or freedom.

Nonetheless, the suggestion that freedom lies in prosperity—not that freedom is the precondition for prosperity—still retains draw. That's mainly because the human heart will always embrace the notion that our shortcomings spring not from choice but from circumstance. Sometimes that's true. But in a free country, it's far more often untrue. Still, that notion relieves us of responsibility while making demands of others. After all, if freedom lies in lack of college debt, then those who demand that you pay your debts are curbing your freedom.

In reality, here's what the #CancelStudentDebt plan would do: continue to drive up the cost of college tuition, with the taxpayer footing that cost. That's precisely what has happened in the past few decades as the feds have involved themselves in the supposedly vital task of ensuring that everyone goes to college. Never mind that many people don't need to go to college—that coming out of college without a skill set but with hundreds of thousands of dollars in debt is a bad bargain. College for all became the mantra; the government stepped into the breach; costs rose. Now government once more steps into the breach.

Canceling student debt may mean a more carefree life for those who voluntarily took on debt, but it means a more burdensome life for those who have paid off their debts, who didn't go to college or who haven't yet been born. And carefree doesn't mean free. It simply means that someone else may be taking responsibility for your decisions. My children are carefree; they're certainly not free.

Going to college is often seen as an important step toward adulthood. Responsible financial decision-making is a far more important step. Disconnecting the two just continues the infantilizing of American adults. But that's all part of Sanders' agenda, isn't it?

Anger for Anger's Sake

July 10, 2019

In the last two weeks, America has learned that a bevy of heretofore relatively uncontroversial objects and ideas are, in fact, extraordinarily controversial. We have learned that the Betsy Ross American flag is irredeemably racist. We have learned that Disney casting a black woman as Ariel in the live-action remake of "The Little Mermaid" is supposedly supremely disquieting for a racist America. We have learned that opposing federally mandated forced busing means that you are a secret bigot, so long as you are named Joe Biden.

Or perhaps we haven't learned any of those things. Perhaps all of this is nonsense, and we've merely learned that Americans are angry, that they're channeling that anger in increasingly bizarre directions, and that opportunists of every stripe are willing to take advantage of that anger for their own benefit.

Take, for example, the Betsy Ross flag. Not only was Ross an abolitionist Quaker; the flag has flown for centuries as a symbol of a country that fought the single bloodiest war in its history to abolish slavery. The flag flew at Barack Obama's inauguration. Not until the last five minutes was someone cloddish enough to suggest that the flag represents slavery and racism—until Nike announced that it had canceled the manufacture of a Ross-inspired shoe at the behest of failed NFL quarterback and national anthem kneeler Colin Kaepernick.

Kaepernick, whose knowledge of politics is approximately as accurate as his downfield passing game, apparently taught Nike some tough lessons about American history (not about sweatshop labor, however). Thus, the sneakers were withdrawn, and a weeklong controversy ensued about the supposed evils of the Ross flag.

The good news for Nike: Its stock rose. That's because Nike knows that controversy generates earned media, and it knows that black Americans are far more likely to be attracted to its social justice warrior posturing *and* more likely to buy more Nike shoes (one study from 1986 to 2002 found that blacks and Hispanics spend up to 30 percent more on apparel and jewelry than whites with comparable incomes).

Corporations understand that nontroversies can sell, just so long as you can sell them as controversies. When Disney announced this month that the actress playing Ariel in its live-action remake of "The Little Mermaid" is Halle Bailey, who is black, a few internet trolls tweeted #NotMyAriel. Soon, the world was aflame with news that the Disney-loving KKK was out of the woodwork; Freeform, a Disney-owned cable channel, immediately unleashed a long open letter "clapping back" at the critics, not a single one of whom was prominent enough to be named.

And in the end, that's how this works: Everyone gets credit for "clapping back," even if there was no actual clapping in the first place.

It works politically, too. The big winner from the first Democratic primary debate was Sen. Kamala Harris, D-Calif., who lumped herself in with Rosa Parks this week after bashing former Vice President Joe Biden for having failed to support federally mandated forced busing in the 1970s. When asked whether she would support such a program, Harris demurred—as, indeed, she had to, since forced busing is wildly unpopular and was wildly unsuccessful, carrying unintended consequences that actually exacerbated de facto segregation rather than alleviating it. She still got points for knocking Biden, though she holds *his exact position* on the issue.

There's a lot of profit to be made, both politically and financially, in generating and maintaining stupid controversy.

Perhaps that speaks to our national need for catharsis. But here's the thing about unjustifiable anger: It's never satiated. So watch for our controversies to get stupider and stupider—and more and more profitable for those who egg them on.

The News Cycle Without Trump's Tweets

July 17, 2019

Let's pretend President Trump didn't tweet.

Let's live in a universe where the president of the United States didn't see fit to insert himself into every controversy, to comment on every passing event, to blast out his inner monologue before tens of millions of Americans each morning—often in the most foolish, controversial or outright xenophobic way—while watching cable news.

Here's what the news cycle would look like.

Last week, House Speaker Nancy Pelosi, D-Calif., went to war with the most famous member of her House contingent, freshman Congresswoman Alexandria Ocasio-Cortez, D-N.Y. After months of vacillating between praise for AOC's supposed energy and put-downs of AOC's radicalism and attacks on moderate Democrats, Pelosi's sneering finally triggered AOC, who promptly brought out her heavy guns: She suggested that Pelosi is a racist targeting congresswomen of color. She even suggested that Pelosi is responsible for the death threats she had received. This, in turn, triggered members of the Congressional Black Caucus to come to Pelosi's defense, and that triggered other members of AOC's so-called squad to come to her defense. By the end of the week, the seething, bubbling war between radicals and mere progressives was threatening to crack the Democratic coalition.

Also last week, Democratic presidential candidates continued their quest to push their party toward the far left. Sen. Kamala

Harris, D-Calif., maintained her hypocritical attacks on former President Joe Biden for his lack of support for federal busing, a policy she herself doesn't support. Sen. Elizabeth Warren, D-Mass., trotted out a new spending plan with no way to pay for it. Harris and Warren prepared to attack each other for attention. Meanwhile, virtually all the major Democratic candidates outside of Biden kept up their drumbeat of criticism of Immigration and Customs Enforcement, demanding an open-borders agenda entirely at odds with the mainstream of American public thought.

This drumbeat came complete with an actual act of violence, as well as a public relations nightmare for the open-borders left. In Washington state, 69-year-old Willem Van Spronsen, armed with a rifle and incendiary devices, attempted to light a car on fire and ignite a propane tank outside a Tacoma migrant detention center to shut it down. He was shot for his trouble. Van Spronsen reportedly called himself a member of antifa, the far-left militant group.

And in Aurora, Colorado, some 2,000 people banded together outside another ICE detention facility, where a group of protesters pulled down the American flag and replaced it with the Mexican flag. Some of the protesters then attempted to burn and deface the American flag with anti-police slurs.

This would seem to have been a pretty decent news cycle for President Trump. The Democratic Party formed itself into a circular firing squad; the far left was busily reminding Americans that it's not especially fond of America altogether.

Then Trump tweeted.

For years, we've heard that Trump's tweeting is a key to his success. There's certainly truth to the notion that Trump is able to redirect the news cycle toward his personal whims based on the click of a few buttons. But with great power comes great risk. When the president decides to tweet, "'Progressive' Democrat Congresswomen ... originally came from countries whose governments are a complete and total catastrophe ... Why don't they go back and help fix the totally broken and crime infested places from which they came," the narrative shifts. The news cycle becomes about Trump's xenophobia (three of the congresswomen he's apparently talking about were born in the United States);

Democrats reunite against him; and the dangers of anti-ICE rhetoric are deliberately obscured by the media.

All too often, Trump's tweets are bad, both morally and politically. And the media would always prefer to jabber about those tweets than about news that harms Democrats. So why would Trump continue to provide them the oxygen they so desperately seek?

Why the Left Is Reconsidering Al Franken

July 24, 2019

On Monday, The New Yorker printed a lengthy piece by reporter Jane Mayer about the sad fate of former Sen. Al Franken, D-Minn. Franken resigned from the Senate in 2017 after a bevy of women accused him of sexual harassment; their accounts ranged from unwanted kisses to unsolicited a-- grabbing. In the midst of the #MeToo movement, Franken stepped down, all the while decrying President Trump's own record of allegations concerning mistreatment of women.

At the time, there were two possible interpretations of events. The first was more inspiring: After decades of defending sexual misconduct by powerful Democratic figures, Democrats and their media allies were finally willing to reset a social standard. In the wake of #MeToo, they had reconsidered their worship of Teddy Kennedy, their pathetic willingness to cover for Bill Clinton. A new day had dawned.

Then there was the second, more cynical theory: Democrats and their media allies were looking to set a new standard out of pure partisanship. They weren't really concerned about Franken's victims any more than they had been about Clinton's victims. Instead, they were looking to establish a level of morally superior ground upon which to attack Trump and demand that Republicans disown him.

This week, we found out which theory was true.

Mayer, the New Yorker reporter, rose to public acclaim just last year when she reported on then-Supreme Court nominee Brett

Kavanaugh's supposed sexual evils. With no supporting facts other than the hazy accounts of decades-old events, she attacked Kavanaugh with alacrity. Now, however, she has flipped: She's concerned with Franken's lack of due process; she questions the political motivations of one of his accusers; she points out that the evidence is supposedly scanty. Democrats, too, have risen to Franken's defense. Many now claim that Sen. Kirsten Gillibrand, D-N.Y., was the real villain in this scenario, having rushed for Franken's scalp precipitously.

In other words, Franken was kicked out of the party when Democrats were trying to build a case against Trump. Now that they've concluded that case won't work, they want Franken back again. Presumably, they'll soon be back to praising Clinton, too.

This sort of behavior is deeply destructive to American public discourse. That's because a standard upheld *only* as a weapon to target political opposition is no standard at all. What's more, the partisan interpretation of the standard creates an incentive for opponents to violate their own commitment to the standard. It's a classic prisoner's dilemma: The person who actually abides by a common moral standard and speaks out against bad behavior on all sides ends up the sucker. Only a fool would call out his own side to the cheers of opponents while his opponents defend their own degenerates.

The problem of politically motivated standards isn't restricted to sexual abuse. It extends to race: Why should Republicans condemn President Trump's tweets about the so-called Squad while Democrats maintain support for Rep. Ilhan Omar's anti-Semitism and Rep. Ayanna Pressley's racism? Why should Republicans provide ammunition to their ill-motivated opponents?

The only way to restore a common standard in politics is for both sides to rebuild trust, step by step. And *that* can only happen when both sides share common goals and values. Otherwise, everyone will decide that losing by abiding by the rules must take a back seat to victory by any means. And that means the destruction of our standards, one by one, until there are no standards left.

We're getting pretty close already.

Baltimore, Land of Political Footballs

July 31, 2019

Back in April 2015, a young black man named Freddie Gray was arrested by the Baltimore Police Department. He'd run from the police, had an illegal knife in his pocket and resisted arrest. The police loaded him into the back of the van but allegedly failed to secure him in place. During the ride to the police station, the van's movement apparently caused Gray to slam his head into one of the walls, resulting in his death.

Given the furor surrounding the deaths of Eric Garner in New York City in July 2014 and Michael Brown in Ferguson, Missouri, in August 2014, among other high-profile deaths of young black men in confrontations with the police, Gray's death quickly spiraled into a national story. Many in Baltimore accused the police of racism and murder.

After Gray's funeral, protests morphed into riots, with 113 police officers injured, 486 people arrested, and serious looting and burning. The mayor of Baltimore at the time, Stephanie Rawlings-Blake, bragged that she had given "space" to "those who wished to destroy." National conversations began over the legacy of racism in Baltimore.

Most of these conversations failed to note that at the time of the incident, the mayor of Baltimore was black; the majority of the city council was black; the police chief was black; the prosecutor against the police was black; three of the charged officers in Gray's case were black; the congressman for the district was black; the president of the United States was black; and the attorney general of the United States was black.

Then, after all of these profound conversations, everything returned to normal in Baltimore: Violent, poverty-stricken, drug-infested (the term "drug-infested" is, by the way, the phraseology of Rep. Elijah Cummings circa 1999, not of President Trump). As of 2018, Baltimore had the highest murder rate of any major American city. That same year, PBS ran a documentary called "Rat Film" about the infestation problem in Baltimore.

Meanwhile, Rawlings-Blake decided not to run for reelection; she had replaced Mayor Sheila Dixon, who had been ousted from office after an embezzlement conviction. Rawlings-Blake was followed by Mayor Catherine Pugh, who resigned amidst allegations of corruption.

The cycle of failure in Baltimore continued.

Then President Trump decided to use Baltimore's failures of governance as a club to wield against Cummings. This was obviously a convenient brickbat: Trump was not proposing a plan for Baltimore or suggesting solutions. But the media determined that Trump's verbiage wasn't merely boorish but racist—and they suggested that Baltimore is, in fact, a thriving urban success. This, of course, is Trump's gift: Anything he touches becomes toxic to Democrats, while anything he criticizes becomes golden.

But when all this is said and done, will Baltimore be any better off?

We all know the answer to that question. The situation in Baltimore requires real solutions, not jabber from either side. Obfuscating Baltimore's problems because Trump put his finger on them doesn't help Baltimore any more than ignoring Baltimore's problems because Democrats govern it. And simply calling out those problems without providing a solution doesn't help Baltimore, either.

Why Can't We Unify in the Face of Evil?

August 7, 2019

This should be easy.

We're all on the same side. When a white supremacist terrorist shoots up a Walmart filled with innocents in El Paso, we should all be on the same side. We should be mourning together; we should be fighting together.

Instead, we're fighting one another.

We're fighting one another for one simple reason: Too many on the political left have become accustomed to castigating the character of those who disagree with the left on policy. Favor tougher border controls? This puts you on the side of the white supremacist terrorist. Believe in Second Amendment rights? You're a vicious, violent cretin covering for those who commit acts of evil. Cite Western civilization as a source of our common values, believe that police forces across the United States are not systemically racist, favor smaller government intervention in the social sphere—in short, disagree with the program of the American left? Most of all, consider voting for Trump? You're an accessory to murder.

Now, there are many on the political left who are too smart for this sort of specious reasoning and character assassination. But not everyone. Charles Blow of The New York Times, for example, writes in a column this week that "terrorists" and "policymakers" are the two "sides of white nationalism." Blow clarifies: "White nationalist terrorists—young and rash—and white nationalist policymakers—older and more methodical—live on parallel planes, both aiming in the same direction, both with the same goal: To maintain and ensure white dominance and white supremacy." Who, pray tell, are these evil white nationalist policymakers? Those who favor "border walls, anti-immigrant laws, voter suppression and packing the courts." Never mind that many advocates of border security also advocate for broader legal immigration. Never mind that nobody actually favors voter suppression. To Blow, an R next to your name signifies merely a less militant Nazism than your neighborhood Hitler Youth.

David Leonhardt of The New York Times similarly argued this week that "American conservatism has a violence problem." While admitting that conservative America "is mostly filled with honorable people who deplore violence and bear no responsibility for right-wing hate killings" and that "liberal America also has violent and deranged people," Leonhardt lays the blame for an increase in political violence at the feet of "mainstream conservative politicians," who are somehow connected to "right-wing extremists."

There's something in the water at The New York Times, obviously. Jamelle Bouie, another voice on The Times opinion page, suggested a "connection between white nationalism" and my personal "ideological project." Never mind that I've been perhaps the loudest voice on the right decrying white nationalism for years; that I firmly fight for particular Western civilized values and small-government conservatism that foreclose and despise racism; that I've incurred hundreds of thousands of dollars in security costs for my trouble; that I require 24/7 security to protect me from white nationalist blowback; and that just weeks ago, the FBI arrested a white nationalist threatening to murder me. Obviously, all conservatives are the same—and all are complicit in the mission of white supremacy.

There can be no unity when one side of the political aisle firmly believes that the other side is motivated by unmitigated evil. No decent conversation about fixes can be had when you assume the person sitting across from you sympathizes with monsters who go to shoot up Hispanic Americans at a Walmart. If we can't at least assume that we're all on the same page in condemning white supremacist terror attacks and white supremacist ideology, we may as well pack this republic in. We're done.

Why We Embrace Conspiracy Theories

August 14, 2019

This week, convicted pedophile Jeffrey Epstein was found unresponsive in his jail cell from an apparent hanging, the day after a court unsealed a cache of documents from a lawsuit against his alleged procurer, Ghislaine Maxwell. Those documents included affidavits from Virginia Roberts Giuffre, the plaintiff, that allege Epstein trafficked her to major figures including former New Mexico Gov. Bill Richardson, Prince Andrew of Britain and former Senate Majority Leader George Mitchell.

Epstein had allegedly attempted suicide in late July, when he apparently tried to hang himself in his cell. He was removed from that cell and placed on suicide watch. Only 11 days before his successful suicide, he was removed from suicide watch.

The failures were systemic. According to the Associated Press, guards on Epstein's unit were "working extreme overtime shifts to make up for staffing shortages." Epstein's jailers were supposed to check on him every 30 minutes but didn't do so, according to The New York Times. Epstein was also supposed to be housed with another inmate so he wasn't alone; that never happened.

Given the public scrutiny on Epstein—he was the most famous federal inmate in custody—it's no wonder that so many Americans are deeply suspicious of his suicide. Epstein had publicly associated with both President Donald Trump and ex-President Bill Clinton; Clinton had flown on Epstein's plane multiple times. Within hours, dueling hashtags #ClintonBodyCount and #TrumpBodyCount trended on Twitter. President Trump, seemingly bothered by the hashtag targeting him, even retweeted Terrence K. Williams: "Died of SUICIDE on 24/7 SUICIDE WATCH? Yeah right! How does that happen ... #JefferyEpstein had information on Bill Clinton & now he's dead ... I see #TrumpBodyCount trending but we know who did this! ... RT if you're not Surprised." Conversely, MSNBC's Joy Reid suggested that Attorney General William Barr, "Trump's consigliere ... whose prime directive is to protect Donald Trump no matter what," might be covering up Epstein's murder.

None of this is good for the country, obviously. But the question is why Americans seem so apt to believe conspiracy theories these days. Some of that certainly has to do with social media, where small pockets of fringe opinion can merge together to create larger pockets of fringe opinion.

Much of it has to do with generalized distrust of the media—distrust that is largely justified by media unwilling to question conspiracism from one side of the aisle. The same weekend Trump idiotically retweeted the Clinton-Epstein conspiracy theory, no less than three Democratic presidential candidates suggested that Michael Brown, the 18-year-old shot by a police officer in Ferguson, Missouri, in 2015 while charging that officer, was actually murdered. Not a single reporter apparently bothered to ask why these candidates were ignoring the report of Barack Obama's Department of Justice, which found no evidence of murder.

More of it has to do with the human inability to accept widespread incompetence. Conspiracies are notoriously difficult to pull off. There are simply too many moving parts. Those who believe in conspiracy theories tend to attribute far more control to human beings than they generally have. Better to believe in conspiracies than to accept the difficult truth that those who are supposed to be able to handle their business often fail at it.

In political terms, though, conspiracism turns up the heat radically. That's because every failure becomes evidence of malevolence on the part of your opponent; every oddity becomes yet another data point in favor of the all-powerful evil of those with whom you disagree.

Better, then, to abide by Hanlon's razor: "Never attribute to malice that which is adequately explained by stupidity." We live in a deeply stupid time. And here's the good news: Stupidity can be handled. Evil is another story.

The Media's Intersectional Embrace of Anti-Semitism

August 21, 2019

Imagine two sitting Republican Congresspeople planned a trip to a foreign country in conjunction with a nongovernmental organization. Imagine that particular NGO had a long history of Jew hatred: It had run a piece on its website quoting anti-Semitic myths about Jews imbibing Christian blood, republished a neo-Nazi article decrying the "Jew-controlled entertainment media" and suggested that "honor" was the proper response to a terrorist who murdered 38 Israelis, including 13 children.

Imagine that these two Congresspeople tweeted a cartoon from a cartoonist so anti-Semitic he won second prize at Iran's Holocaust denial cartoon contest. Imagine that these Congresspeople had themselves engaged in anti-Semitic slurs, ranging from a suggestion that Israel supporters in America suffer from dual loyalty, to the accusation that Israel "hypnotized the world," to the suggestion that Jewish money lies behind America's support for Israel ("it's all about the Benjamins"). Imagine that these Congresspeople had expressed support for terrorist Rasmea Odeh. Imagine also that both Congresspeople had a long history of associations with open anti-Semites.

Finally, imagine that both members were supporters of the anti-Semitic boycott, divest and sanctions (BDS) movement directed against Israel—a movement so obviously anti-Semitic that a bipartisan coterie ranging from Sen. Ted Cruz, R-T., to House Speaker Nancy Pelosi, D-Calif., had declared it so.

Now imagine that these two Republican Congresspeople were barred from entering Israel under Israel's law that prevents propagandizing designed to destroy the state of Israel. Would the media report on Israel's reaction or on the Republican Congresspeople's associations, actions and statements? Would the narrative surround Israel's supposed free speech crackdown, or would it center on the obvious Jew hatred of the Republican Congresspeople?

And yet.

Simply switch out the word "Republican" for "Democrat" and the media coverage shifts 180 degrees. Suddenly, the Congresspeople become put-upon heroes, victimized by the evils of the nefarious Jewish state. Suddenly, a media blackout arises with regard to the NGO sponsoring the visit; the Washington Post calls the organization "a nonprofit organization headed by Palestinian lawmaker and longtime peace negotiator Hanan Ashrawi"; The New York Times praises the group for raising "global awareness and knowledge of Palestinian realities." The statements of the Congresspeople become mere conversation starters; The New York Times praises one for starting a vital conversation about Israel. The BDS position becomes worthy of debate, rather than a symptom of anti-Semitism.

Our major media are driven by narrative, not by fact. And the narrative depends on the players. Congresswomen Ilhan Omar, D-Minn., and Rashida Tlaib, D-Mich., aren't hiding their anti-Semitism. They revel in it. And why not? The media celebrate them as "The Squad." Pelosi cowers before them. And their anti-Semitic propaganda receives kid-glove treatment.

And Omar and Tlaib aren't new. Media coverage of Israel has long been skewed in favor of Israel's enemies. How much coverage, for example, has the mainstream media given to the Palestinian Authority's announcement—this week—that an LGBTQ group would be banned in its territories, since the PA's values are in conflict with those of the group? The answer: virtually none. As of this writing, hardly any pieces have appeared in a non-Jewish or non-conservative publication.

Jews simply aren't part of the intersectional narrative, unless they are targeted by those perceived as higher on the scale of privilege. It's that simple and that despicable. It's the reason Rev. Al Sharpton has a show on MSNBC, the reason Democratic politicians continue to play footsie with Louis Farrakhan, the reason The New York Times ignores hate crimes in its own city, the reason Omar and Tlaib are treated as victims rather than pariahs. All of which underscores just why Israel seeks to protect itself so strongly from those who seek to destroy her: There are plenty of people out there who want to, and our media watchdogs are too busy drooling over them to remember that their job is to report the news.

Trump Is Right on the China Threat

August 28, 2019

President Trump's latest foray into the world of international economics—his ongoing trade war with China—has been widely derided by his critics. It's been derided on the grounds that there is no long-term strategy; on the grounds that the trade war will not be, as Trump has bragged, "good and easy to win"; on the grounds that Trump continues to send mixed signals, simultaneously claiming that China is bearing the brunt of his tariffs while desperately urging Federal Reserve Chairman Jerome Powell to lower interest rates.

Now, Trump's trade policy may not be well-considered. His understanding of trade is rudimentary at best—he still operates under the assumption that mutually beneficial trade is actually a zero-sum game. And Trump's rhetoric may be confusing—it's unclear whether Trump wants tariffs or wants to alleviate them. But Trump does have one thing absolutely right: China is an imperturbable geopolitical foe. And the United States ought to be taking a serious look at a long-term strategy to contain and then reverse the dominance of the totalitarian communist regime.

Trump is the only president of recent vintage to understand this simple truth. The Chinese regime is strengthening its totalitarianism; market forces have not opened up China's politics. China's attempts to strengthen its grip on Hong Kong, its forays into the complexities of Indian-Pakistani politics, its threats of sanctions against American firms over the sale of jets to Taiwan—all of this bespeaks the intent of the Xi Jinping regime, which has a philosophy of political revanchism. The supposed moderation of Dengism—the political philosophy of Deng Xiaoping, which supposedly prized pragmatism over doctrinal adherence to Marxist tenets—is being quickly reversed, with China's economy placed at the mercy of political leadership. Dengism was always treated with too much optimism by the West: The same regime supposedly pushing for detente with the West stole hundreds of billions in intellectual property every year for years while continuing to build up its military. Still, Xi has moved away from even tepid moves toward openness.

Two significant projects in recent years demonstrate the scale of China's ambitions. First, there's the so-called Belt and Road Initiative, in which China has helped subsidize building infrastructure in a bevy of countries throughout the world. Up to 68 countries are already taking part. The project is designed to place these countries in hock to the Chinese government; it's also designed to maximize China's naval power in the region.

Then there is China's heavy focus on government-subsidized building of 5G, using Huawei as the tip of the spear. China is offering 5G technology to developing countries at discounted prices, and those countries, hungry for the technology, have been accepting, likely at the cost of their own privacy and security. The goal, as always: maximization of China's sphere of influence.

Free trade isn't going to cure this. China's government has been willing to utilize mercantilism to prop up its global ambitions. Capitalism hasn't opened China's politics. Free trade has indeed benefitted China's citizens, bringing hundreds of millions out of poverty, but the Chinese government has responded with more repression, not less. All of which means that the United States must be pursuing a thorough strategy of opposition to China's ambitions.

Trump seems to understand this. But if he fails to articulate that to the American people, his economic war with China will fail. That's because if the American people are asked to shoulder an economic burden without being informed as to the rationale or the cost, they will rightly buck. Trump hasn't explained that the burden exists, let alone why the American people should shoulder it.

With that said, at least Trump recognizes the threat China represents. The chattering class has, for far too long, ignored that threat, to the detriment of the United States and her allies.

How the Quest for Power Corrupted Elizabeth Warren

September 4, 2019

I first met Elizabeth Warren when she was a professor at Harvard Law School, in 2004. She was fresh off the publication of her bestselling book, "The Two-Income Trap." There's no doubt she was politically liberal—our only face-to-face meeting involved a recruitment visit at the W Hotel in Los Angeles, where she immediately made some sort of disparaging remark about Rush Limbaugh—but at the time, Warren was making waves for her iconoclastic views. She wasn't a doctrinaire leftist, spewing Big Government nostrums. She was a creative thinker.

That creative thinking is obvious in "The Two-Income Trap," which discusses the rising number of bankruptcies among middle-class parents, particularly women with children. The book posits that women entered the workforce figuring that by doing so, they could have double household income. But so many women entered the workforce that they actually inflated prices for basic goods like housing, thus driving debt skyward and leading to bankruptcies for two-income families. The book argued that families with one income might actually be better off, since families with two incomes spent nearly the full combined income and then fell behind if one spouse lost a job. Families with one income, by contrast, spent to the limit for one income, and if a spouse was fired, the unemployed spouse would then look for work to replace that single income.

Warren's core insight was fascinating: She argued that massive expansion of the labor force had actually created more stressful living and driven down median wages. But her policy recommendations were even more fascinating. She explicitly argued against "more government regulation of the housing market," slamming "complex regulations," since they "might actually worsen the situation by diminishing the incentive to build new houses or improve older ones." Instead, she argued in favor of school choice, since pressure on housing prices came largely from families seeking to escape badly run government school districts: "A well-designed voucher program would fit the bill neatly."

Her heterodox policy proposals didn't stop there. She refused to "join the chorus calling for taxpayer-funded day care" on its own, calling it a "sacred cow." At the very least, she suggested that "government-subsidized day care would add one more indirect pressure on mothers to join the workforce." She instead sought a more comprehensive educational solution that would include "tax credits for stay-at-home parents."

She ardently opposed additional taxpayer subsidization of college loans, too, or more taxpayer spending on higher education directly. Instead, she called for a tuition freeze from state schools. She recommended tax incentives for families to save rather than spend. She opposed radical solutions wholesale: "We haven't suggested a complete overhaul of the tax structure, and we haven't demanded that businesses cease and desist from ever closing another plant or firing another worker. Nor have we suggested that the United States should build a quasi-socialist safety net to rival the European model."

So, what happened to Warren?

Power.

The other half of iconoclastic Warren was typical progressive, anti-financial industry Warren. In "The Two-Income Trap," she proposes reinstating state usury laws, cutting off access to payday lenders and heavily regulating the banking industry—all in the name of protecting Americans from themselves. While her position castigating the credit industry for deliberate obfuscation of clients was praiseworthy, her quest to "protect consumers" quickly morphed into a quest to create the Consumer Finance Protection Bureau—an independent agency without any serious checks or balances. But despite her best efforts, she never became head of the CFPB, failing to woo Republican senators. The result: an emboldened Warren who saw her popularity as tied to her Big Government agenda. No more reaching across the aisle; no more iconoclastic policies. Instead, she would be Ralph Nader II, with a feminist narrative to boot.

And so, she's gaining ground in the 2020 presidential race as a Bernie Sanders knockoff. Ironically, her great failing could be her lack of moderation—the moderation she abandoned in her quest for progressive power. If Elizabeth Warren circa 2003 were running, she'd be the odds-on favorite for president. But Warren circa 2019 would hate Warren circa 2003.

Did We Learn the Lesson of 9/11?

September 11, 2019

It's now been nearly a full generation since Sept. 11, 2001. There are people currently serving in the U.S. military who weren't born when that act of evil took place—and the military still has thousands of troops in Afghanistan, the home base of the Taliban-supported al Qaida attack on the United States that took nearly 3,000 American lives.

With time comes forgetfulness. The same period of time has now elapsed since Sept. 11 that elapsed between the end of World War I (1918) and the German re-occupation of the Rhineland in contravention of the Treaty of Versailles (1936). Believing that World War I had ended all war, the Allied powers did nothing. That same year, Germany concluded its Axis alliance with Italy, as well as its Anti-Comintern Pact with Japan. Less than three years later, the world would be at war.

Forgetfulness is easy, because immediate costs are painful and steep. American foreign policy nearly always vacillates between two poles: isolationism and reactive interventionism. The American people (correctly) don't like the consequences of isolationism—increased attacks on America and her allies, maximization of influence by our enemies—but we also dislike (correctly) the consequences of maintaining a global military presence. It was easy to tear into the Clinton administration's weakness on defense in the aftermath of the Cold War, but there was almost no political cost in it for Clinton at the time. The sepia glow of media coverage regarding Barack Obama hasn't been darkened by his single-minded quest to minimize American influence around the world.

But every so often, we're reminded that the world is filled with enemies.

We were reminded of that unfortunate fact this week when President Trump withdrew an apparently secret invitation to the Taliban to visit Camp David. The Taliban was, is and will remain an Islamic terror group; it has continuously sought the murder of American soldiers and citizens for two decades. Why would the Trump administration think it a good idea to sign an agreement with radicals who seek to overthrow the administration of Afghanistan, support terrorism and despise the United States? Do members of the administration truly believe that any agreement signed by the Taliban will be binding?

The answer, of course, is no. That's why the talks fell apart, according to The New York Times—a response from inside the administration in the aftermath of a terror attack on American soldiers this week, a recognition of the obvious.

The problem, of course, is that there are no easy solutions when it comes to foreign policy in the worst parts of the world. Everyone of good heart wants American soldiers out of Afghanistan and home. But how many Americans are willing to risk the increase in terrorism likely to follow such a withdrawal?

So long as we remember 9/11, the answer will be: very few.

Now, perhaps we should withdraw from Afghanistan. Perhaps the withdrawal is worth the risk. But American history isn't replete with circumstances in which precipitous withdrawal is followed by peace and security.

All of which means that American troops are likely to remain in Afghanistan for the foreseeable future. Few politicians will be bold enough to simply state that truth. After all, when John McCain said as much in 2008, he was roundly mocked by Barack Obama—the same Obama who escalated the war in Afghanistan and retained thousands of troops there, despite promising withdrawal repeatedly. But our politicians should be brave enough to recognize that a weaker America on the world stage means a more vulnerable America at home. If we didn't learn that lesson on 9/11, we're bound to repeat it.

The Alternative History of the United States

September 18, 2019

Last week, Democrats held their first true presidential debate. With the field winnowed down to 10 candidates—three of them actual contenders for the nomination—only one moment truly stood out. That moment came not from Joe Biden, Elizabeth Warren or Bernie Sanders but from a candidate desperate for attention: Beto O'Rourke.

O'Rourke ran in 2018 for a Senate seat in Texas and lost in shockingly narrow fashion to incumbent Republican Sen. Ted Cruz. But his persona at the time was more Biden than Bernie: He ran as a unifying quasi-moderate, an Obama-esque figure determined to bring Americans together. In the early going of the presidential race, Beto was figured to be a prime contender: An April poll showed him in a solid third place. But he's faded dramatically; now the once-media darling is polling below 3 percent.

So O'Rourke has refashioned himself into a woke warrior. He's declared that he wants to forcibly remove guns from law-abiding Americans ("Hell, yes, we're going to take your AR-15"), that President Trump is a "white supremacist" posing a "mortal threat to people of color" and that the time has come for race reparations. Most dramatically, O'Rourke has refashioned his vision of American history. In this debate, he laid out his retelling of the American story, saying: "Racism in America is endemic. It is foundational. We can mark the creation of this country not at the Fourth of July, 1776, but Aug. 20, 1619, when the first kidnapped African was brought to this country against his will and in bondage, and as a slave built the greatness and the success and the wealth that neither he nor his descendants would ever be able to fully participate in and enjoy."

This version of history is cribbed from "The 1619 Project" by The New York Times, a retelling of American history as a story rooted in white supremacy—not colored by or affected by white supremacy but rooted in it. Capitalism, criminal justice, lack of universal health care, traffic patterns, Donald Trump's election—all of it, according to "The 1619 Project," is fundamentally based on America's legacy of slavery and racial discrimination.

That perspective on American history, in turn, is merely warmed over Howard Zinn. Zinn, the Marxist author of "A People's History of the United States," sought to recast America's story as a story of hideous ugliness covered with the hypocritical facade of goodness. Never mind that "A People's History" is, in fact, rotten history—factually inaccurate, wildly disjoined from a more comprehensive examination of time and place, near plagiarized from the work of better leftist historians. Zinn's history has now infused the teaching of American history in high schools and colleges across the country.

But that historical retelling is at odds with the better, truer story of America: the story of a nation founded on eternally good and true principles, principles only fully realized for many Americans at the cost of blood and sweat and death. Ex-slave Frederick Douglass's take on American history remains the most honest, as well as the most visionary. While acknowledging that to the American slave, Independence Day represents "more than all other days in the year, the gross injustice and cruelty to which he is the constant victim," Douglass recognized that the Constitution is a "glorious liberty document," the Declaration of Independence a charter of "saving principles."

American history *is* our common history. O'Rourke's pathetic rewriting of American history is designed not to unify us as a nation but to divide us—to call us away from the unifying principles that lie at the foundation of America, in favor of divisive principles of tribal partisanship. We *must* recognize the evils of American history—that is part of our common story. In fact, our quest to rid ourselves of those evils *is* our common story. But if we wish to survive as a nation, we must also recognize that the story of America lies in the constant purification of our actions to align *with* our founding principles, not oppose them.

Catastrophic Thinking Without Solutions

September 27, 2019

In July, Adam Grant, organizational psychologist at Wharton Business School, tweeted: "Agendas aren't driven by problems. They're driven by solutions. Calling out what's wrong without proposing ways to make it right is complaining."

This week, complaining was the order of the day.

The complaining was largely done by enthusiastic minors, to the raucous applause of Democratic politicians and the media. Greta Thunberg, a 16-year-old activist from Sweden, appeared before a UN climate summit to chide the adults in catastrophic terms usually reserved for bad B-disaster flicks: "You have stolen my dreams and my childhood with your empty words. ... We are at the beginning of a mass extinction, and all you can talk about is money and fairy tales of eternal economic growth. How dare you?" One student intoned at a weekend rally, "All of our futures are in jeopardy." Another student said, "We will be the last generation to survive."

This, of course, is nonsense. We will not be the last generation to survive. The world will keep on spinning. The damage from climate change is uncertain—it may be moderate, and it may be graver. But to suggest, as ralliers did, that the world will end without ACTION! (no specific action recommended) is factually untrue.

All of this "activism" prompted former President Barack Obama to tweet his kudos: "One challenge will define the future for today's young generation more dramatically than any other: Climate change. The millions of young people worldwide who've organized and joined today's #ClimateStrike demand action to protect our planet, and they deserve it."

What action, precisely? And why is the left so keen on rallying behind children to push their cause, the same way it did with regard to gun control in the aftermath of the Parkland shooting?

Perhaps it's because we don't expect children to have solutions. After all, they're children. But adults hiding behind children to avoid the difficult conversations that must take place about how to achieve solutions is nothing other than moral cowardice. At the same time leftist politicians were rooting on these children, commending them for their exuberance, the United Nations was accomplishing nothing on the issue of climate change. That's because the lead emitters on planet Earth aren't in the West. They're in China and India. And as The New York Times reported, "despite the protests in the streets, China on Monday made no new promises to take stronger climate action." Western teenagers screaming in front of cameras aren't going to convince Chinese President Xi Jinping to lower emissions and join in a global carbon tax. Hell, Hong Kong teenagers shutting down airports can't convince Xi to not violate international agreements.

It turns out that complaining without solutions isn't actually useful—at least if you're interested in solving problems. It's political pandering, designed to make solutions more difficult by adding moral condemnation to political infeasibility. That merely frustrates people with the "system," since such pandering falsely suggests that at the heart of the problem lies cruel apathy—and apathy directed at crying children—rather than serious political gridlock. It's divisive, rather than unifying, and polarizing, rather than practical.

But perhaps that's the point, at least for the adults who take advantage of children to hide behind their own unwillingness to acknowledge the difficult realities of solution-making.

Impeachment Isn't Merited

October 2, 2019

President Trump is a bull in a china shop. He says inadvisable things to inadvisable people, mainly because he is inadvisable—literally no one can advise him. The vast majority of things Trump says are ignored or brushed off by those who understand the difference between bloviation and manipulation. Still, Trump's constant stream of noise can make it difficult to tell the difference between the two.

So when an intelligence community whistleblower came forward with an allegation that, on a call with the Ukrainian president, Trump proposed a quid pro quo with the Ukrainian government—release of military aid in exchange for a Ukrainian investigation into Joe Biden and son Hunter Biden—the allegation didn't appear absurd on its face. The timeline, after all, seemed to match up: Trump allegedly suspended military aid to Ukraine personally a week before talking with the Ukrainian president, only to release the aid after the holdup was met with public scrutiny.

Then, the Trump administration released a transcript of the call, in which Trump used the typical New York real estate wheeler-dealer language of favors: favors related to investigations surrounding CrowdStrike, the firm tasked with analyzing the hack of the Democratic National Committee in 2016, an investigation that concluded with allegations of Russian interference; favors related to helping Rudy Giuliani investigate the origins of the 2016 Trump-

Russia investigation; favors related to investigating the Bidens. The theory seemed to be gaining credibility.

Then it seemed to fall apart. It turned out that the Ukrainian government apparently had no clue that Trump was even withholding military aid—and without such a *quid*, there couldn't be a *pro quo*. The Ukrainian president publicly proclaimed that Trump hadn't pressured him. The whistleblower report turned out to be third-hand gossip rather than first-hand information. And allegations of a cover-up imploded as the Trump administration released information ranging from the transcript to the whistleblower report itself.

And so, Democrats have begun to move the goalposts. Now Democrats are claiming that the State Department is engaged in obstruction, just minutes after claiming that Trump's Department of Justice had engaged in obstruction. Democrats allege that Trump's behavior—without allegations of criminal conduct—is enough to justify impeachment. Now, after Trump predictably took to Twitter to rail against the whistleblower and the Democrats, Democrats claim his behavior amounts to "witness intimidation."

As the grounds for the impeachment inquiry broaden, it's becoming clear that the Democrats' enthusiasm for impeachment outweighed their supporting evidence. They leapt before they looked—and now they're trying to backfill an impeachment inquiry that must end with an impeachment vote or lay bare the emptiness of the original attacks themselves.

Perhaps Democrats *will* come up with something. That's always possible, given the amount of leaking and loose talk around the White House. But barring some sort of cataclysmic revelation, the impeachment effort seems to be stalling out. And based on the current evidence, it should.

The NBA Proves That Corporate Social Activism Is All About the Dollars

October 9, 2019

In recent years, the NBA has become famously political. During the heyday of the Black Lives Matter movement, the NBA permitted players to wear slogan-printed T-shirts in support, and stars like LeBron James, Dwyane Wade and Chris Paul spoke out loudly on the issue. The Sacramento Kings actually announced a partnership with the local branch of the movement. And NBA players have had little problem denouncing President Trump, whom James called a "bum." In 2017, Commissioner Adam Silver actually tried to blackmail the city of Charlotte, North Carolina, by pulling the All-Star Game, all in an attempt to restore the so-called "bathroom bill" for transgender people.

The NBA has reaped the benefit from its benevolent attitude toward left-leaning social activism, too. Silver, like former Commissioner David Stern before him, has been praised ad infinitum by the press, compared favorably to that alleged corporate hobgoblin Roger Goodell of the NFL. Silver told CNN just last year that "part of being an NBA player" is social activism and a "sense of an obligation, social responsibility, a desire to speak up directly about issues that are important." Silver stated the league wants players to "be multi-dimensional people and fully participate as citizens." He specifically explained that the league had a role in ensuring that the situation remains "safe" for players afraid of suffering career blowback.

Then the NBA came up against its own corporate interests.

And the NBA caved.

Late last week, Houston Rockets general manager Daryl Morey tweeted an eminently uncontroversial statement: "Fight for freedom, stand with Hong Kong." That's about as milquetoast a statement about Hong Kong as it's possible to make. But that didn't matter to the Chinese government, which immediately stated that it would cut relations with the NBA and the Rockets in particular. Speculation quickly ran rampant that Morey might lose his job. Morey was forced to delete his tweet and walk it back: "I did not intend my tweet to cause any offense to Rockets fans and friends of mine in China. I was merely voicing one thought, based on one interpretation, of one complicated event. I have had a lot of opportunity since that tweet to hear and consider other perspectives." James Harden, star of the team, tweeted, "We apologize. We love China. We love playing there." Silver's NBA put out an apology in Chinese saying (as translated), "We are extremely disappointed in the inappropriate comment by the general manager of the Houston Rockets."

So, what happened to all of that corporate do-gooderism? It simply disappeared upon contact with reality. That's the sad truth of corporate politics: If it takes kowtowing to the Chinese communist government to earn a quick dollar, corporations will do it. Ask Google. Or Hollywood studios. Or the NBA.

All of which gives the lie to the bizarre notion that corporations are handmaidens for capitalist exploitation. They're not. They simply follow dollars. If they can grab those dollars through cronyism with governments, they will. In fact, that's easier than retaining a competitive advantage in a free and open marketplace.

There's another, more important point at stake. When corporations virtue signal to the left, they're doing so for the same reason the NBA just bowed to China: dollars. The NBA understands that American leftists are far more censorious than conservatives—and that means that openly pandering to the American left earns product loyalty from that political contingent, without serious consequences from American conservatives. It's not about pure principle for Adam Silver and company—or for any other newly woke corporations discovering their inner social activists. It's about the green. It always is.

Beto Says the Quiet Part out Loud

October 16, 2019

Failing Democratic presidential candidate Beto O'Rourke is raging against the dying of his political light. Desperate and alone, his campaign on the precipice of collapse, Beto has banked on one policy: radical honesty. And that means he is now saying the quiet part of the progressive agenda out loud. This is a candidate who openly claims he'll come take Americans' guns (though he then pretends this won't involve the police acting as an enforcement arm in removing those weapons). This is a candidate who suggests that abortion one day before full term is a constitutional right.

And now this is a candidate who admits that he will seek to bankrupt virtually every traditional religious institution in America.

When asked at a CNN Democratic town hall regarding LGBTQ issues about whether nonprofit status should be removed from churches that refuse to honor same-sex marriages, O'Rourke simply said, "Yes." He then explained in detail: "There can be no reward, no benefit, no tax break for anyone, or any institution, any organization in America that denies the full human rights and the full civil rights of every single one of us. ... And so as president we are going to make that a priority, and we are going to stop those who are infringing upon the rights of our fellow Americans."

This statement is insanely radical. It suggests that the mere presence of religious institutions that dissent from the social left's political orthodoxy cannot be tolerated. It is not an infringement on rights for free associations of religious people to deny the validity of marriages based on both historic natural law and traditionally religious precepts. But according to O'Rourke, the existence of such institutions amounts to an infringement.

This move by O'Rourke was utterly foreseeable. In expectation of precisely this sort of logic, I endorsed the libertarian position on same-sex marriage—get government out of the entire business of marriage—in March 2013, two years before Obergefell v. Hodges. I wrote at the time that any federal cramdown of same-sex marriage would result in states being "forced to recognize same-sex marriages," public schools being forced to teach its morality and religious institutions losing tax-exempt status. "Religious Americans," I predicted, "will be forced into violating their beliefs or facing legal consequences by the government. The First Amendment guarantee of religious liberty will largely become obsolete."

At the time, this was considered over-the-top. Now it's a mainstream Democratic position.

And the Democrats will go further than merely removing nonprofit status. They will use anti-discrimination law as a baton to destroy the existence of "discriminatory" religious institutions, from churches to synagogues to religious schools. They will refuse to accredit home-schooling programs that do not teach the left's preferred social values—after all, anything less would be benefitting organizations that, in O'Rourke's view, deny "the full human rights" of LGBTQ people.

This tyrannical thinking was expressly prohibited by the founders, who saw the threat of government toward religion as paramount—not the other way around. And for years, Democrats have understood that O'Rourke's agenda had to be kept under wraps—most Americans aren't interested in his full-scale culture war.

But now he's saying the quiet part out loud. It will be fascinating—and frightening—to see how many Democrats echo him in the coming months.

The 'Lynching' Controversy and the Death of Common Language

October 23, 2019

In the Bible, the people of Babel unite in fighting God; they decide to build a massive tower to challenge God's supremacy. God, annoyed by their presumption, promptly causes them to speak a variety of tongues, dividing them and ending the foolhardy project.

The story represents a simple truth: unity relies, at least in large part, on shared language.

In the United States, we're watching our shared language disintegrate.

On Tuesday, President Donald Trump fired off one of his infamously impassioned tweets about the Democrats' impeachment inquiry. Frustrated by Democrats' lack of clarity on process with regard to that inquiry, Trump wrote: "So some day, if a Democrat becomes President and the Republicans win the House, even by a tiny margin, they can impeach the President, without due process or fairness or any legal rights. All Republicans must remember what they are witnessing here—a lynching. But we will WIN!"

Trump's use of the word "lynching" immediately set off a firestorm. Characteristic among denunciations was one from former Vice President Joe Biden, who imperiously intoned: "Our country has a dark, shameful history with lynching, and to even think about making this comparison is abhorrent. It's despicable."

There was just one problem: Biden used the exact same language in October 1998 to describe the Clinton impeachment. "History is going to question whether or not this was just a partisan lynching," Biden said back then. Which prompted Biden—today's Biden—to condemn himself, stating: "That wasn't the right word to use and I'm sorry about that. Trump on the other hand chose his words deliberately today in his use of the word lynching and continues to stoke racial divides in this country daily."

Oh.

So when Joe Biden used the word "lynching" to describe his perception of a politically motivated impeachment in 1998, that was merely poor word choice. When Trump used it in 2019, he obviously meant to liken himself to black victims of white supremacist violence.

Or, alternatively, everyone is full of it.

Politics is wildly skewing our use of basic language. And that phenomenon is one of the key factors tearing apart the country. Every word becomes a potential dog whistle. Every phrase is parsed by the politically motivated for signs of malign intent. Politically correct language policing becomes the order of the day. Misunderstanding becomes malice; clarity becomes confusion.

The deliberate confusion fostered regarding gender pronouns is yet another example of this phenomenon. It is not a sign of malice to suggest that gender pronouns refer to objective measures of sex. It is a sign of a delusional culture to suggest that third party use of gender pronouns must refer instead to subjective self-identification. Yet we are told that virtue mandates that we pretend that transgender women *are* women, even if that means that biological men compete with biological women in sport; we are told that virtue requires that parents call their confused 7-year-olds by their chosen pronouns, even though confused children desperately require guidance, love and advice from parents, not mere affirmation of malleable self-identification.

We cannot have conversations with one another if we refuse to define terms. But refusal to define terms is one of the most fruitful methods of impugning others. If we seek division rather than unity, we'll certainly find it. And as we cordon ourselves off into separate interpretations of language we once held in common, we're less and less likely to ever again find common ground.

The J Street Democrats

October 30, 2019

This week, four of the top candidates for the 2020 Democratic presidential nomination—Pete Buttigieg, Amy Klobuchar, Julian Castro and Bernie Sanders—gathered at the J Street Conference to explain why the United States ought to pressure the state of Israel to make concessions to terrorists, why the Obama administration was correct to appease the Iranian regime and why American Jews ought to value the opinions of Bernie Sanders over those of Israeli Prime Minister Benjamin Netanyahu on the future of Jewish safety. Two other top Democrats—Elizabeth Warren and Joe Biden—sent video messages in support of the group.

By contrast, when the American Israel Public Affairs Committee held its annual conference in March, not a single Democratic presidential candidate showed up. The Democrats are, by and large, simply too ashamed to stand with an actual pro-Israel group, although prominent congressional leaders still show up to mouth nostrums about bipartisan support for Israel.

But the heart of the Democratic Party has moved against Israel. That's because Israel is economically successful, while its enemies are not; Israel is liberal, while its enemies are not; Israel is the tip of the spear of Western civilization in an area known for its tribalism and brutality. This means that according to the radical left, Israel is an exploitative country hell-bent on domination, despite its lack of territorial ambition—Israel has signed over large swaths of land won through military victory to geopolitical enemies, and offered much more repeatedly.

So the Democrats built up and gave credence to J Street, a Trojan horse group dedicated to undermining American support for Israel and justifying left-wing hatred of the Jewish state. J Street was founded by Clinton operative Jeremy Ben-Ami and Israeli far-left political figure Daniel Levy in late 2007. One of its chief sources of funding—a source obscured in the early years by its founders—was anti-Israel radical George Soros.

The media quickly began treating J Street as a legitimate representative of mainstream Jewish opinion on Israel, and so did Democrats, particularly in the anti-Israel Obama administration: Rather than having to deal with those troublesome *actually* pro-Israel voices at AIPAC, it was easier to bring in a few ringers from J Street to pretend that advocating for negotiations with Hamas represented an acceptable opinion in the pro-Israel community.

And those sorts of positions routinely crop up at J Street. J Street repeatedly urged the Obama administration to abstain from anti-Israel resolutions at the United Nations. Proponents of the anti-Semitic Boycott, Divestment and Sanctions movement have found comfort at their events. J Street was an adamant backer of Barack Obama's Iran deal when the pro-Israel community unanimously opposed it. J Street has refused to condemn a government deal between the Palestinian Authority and Hamas and has even undermined Israeli self-defense in conflicts with Hamas. On campus, J Street regularly hosts groups dedicated to smearing the Israel Defense Forces.

So it was no wonder that Bernie Sanders arrived at the J Street conference and quickly suggested aid to Israel be redirected to the Gaza Strip, run by Hamas, to the cheers of attendees. It was no surprise when Buttigieg suggested that the Iran deal correctly ignored Iran's terrorist funding and ballistic missile testing, while also suggesting that America reconsider aid to Israel if Israel continues to build in disputed areas of Judea and Samaria. It was no shock when Julian Castro pledged to open an embassy in East Jerusalem for the Palestinians—despite the fact that no solution has been negotiated with regard to the final status of Jerusalem.

Leaders in the Democratic Party may maintain that their anti-Israel turn is due to Benjamin Netanyahu. Those who understand Israeli politics know better. There is wide consensus in Israel that no negotiation can be expected with Hamas, Islamic jihadis or the Palestinian Authority; those negotiations have ended in blood too many times. Absent a peace partner, there can be no peace. Democrats must know this. But they'd prefer to blind themselves to that knowledge—and use J Street to cover their tracks.

Is Elizabeth Warren Set to Fall?

November 6, 2019

This has been an awful week for the purported new 2020 Democratic presidential front-runner, Sen. Elizabeth Warren, D-Mass. For months, Warren has received nearly unmitigated praise from the media for her bevy of "plans." She's been praised as "wonkish" and "brainy" and "focused." Her growth in the polls has been the dual result of a strong organizational effort by her campaign in early primary states like Iowa and New Hampshire, and endless gobs of drool from reporters.

But now the bloom is coming off the rose.

For months, Warren has simply lied about whether she would raise middle-class taxes to pay for her Bernie Sanders-lite proposal to replace America's health care insurance system with "Medicare for All." To support that lie, on Friday, she released another one of her now-famous plans. It is a compendium of tissue-thin falsehoods, a plan about as plausible as Rep. Alexandria Ocasio-Cortez's Green New Deal. According to Warren's plan, she'll somehow manage to institute a wildly generous Medicare For All policy—including coverage for illegal immigrants—at a one-third discount off virtually all major estimates. She'll radically reduce reimbursement rates for doctors and hospitals—and yet, care levels won't suffer. She'll cram down drugmakers' prescription drug prices—but innovation won't suffer. She'll jack up taxes on the wealthy—but the wealthy won't engage in tax avoidance.

The plan is a joke. It's a lie.

But that's Warren's tendency: dishonest radicalism. At least Sen. Sanders, I-Vt., can be counted on to tell the unfortunate truth about soaking the middle class. Warren can be counted on to shift her policy proposals to appease specific constituencies and then lie about how she'll pay for them. She'll also lie about everything from her own ethnicity (Harvard Law School graduate David French rightly calls Warren an "academic grifter") to her research on medical bankruptcy (she has claimed that "medical bankruptcies" represent a far higher percentage of all bankruptcies than can be supported by the facts).

All of this underscores her unelectability. As her poll numbers have risen, so, too, has Democrats' wishcasting that perhaps—just perhaps—her unelectability has been overestimated. Maybe, the argument goes, voters aren't put off by Warren's radicalism and tendency toward scolding self-righteousness. Maybe Warren can pull this thing off.

Also last Friday, a poll came from The New York Times and Siena College. It pitted former Vice President Joe Biden, Sanders and Warren against President Trump in the battleground states and showed that among likely voters, Warren trails Trump in every major battleground state. She's down by four points in Michigan, two in Pennsylvania, two in Wisconsin, four in Florida and four in North Carolina. Biden, by comparison, is up in all of those states except North Carolina.

And Warren's numbers are likely to drop. Remember, Trump's numbers aren't particularly malleable. Neither are Biden's, since he has 100% name recognition. Warren, however, isn't widely known by the public. That means Trump—whose chief political skill lies in his willingness to use every iota of dirt against political opponents—will have the opportunity to define Warren. If she's riding weak against Trump now, wait until he dubs her "Lieawatha."

All of which explains why Warren has been faring worse in national polling of late. In early October, Warren actually surpassed Biden in the RealClearPolitics poll average of national numbers. Now she's down nearly double digits again.

So hold the phone on that inevitable Warren nomination. Warren's a weak front-runner. And she's not getting any stronger.

Are Conservative Immigration Restrictionists Racist?

November 13, 2019

This week, The Atlantic released its newest issue, provocatively titled "How to Stop a Civil War." Leading its collection of essays is a fascinating piece by Yoni Applebaum. In it, Applebaum posits that at the crux of America's vitriolic politics lies demographic change: "The United States is undergoing a transition perhaps no rich and stable democracy has ever experienced: Its historically dominant group is on its way to becoming a political minority—and its minority groups are asserting their co-equal rights and interests." This, he suggests, has led to an impasse for the center-right, which refuses to adapt to changing demographics, instead doubling down on President Donald Trump's white, working-class base. Applebaum explains, "When a group that has traditionally exercised power comes to believe that its eclipse is inevitable, and that the destruction of all it holds dear will follow, it will fight to preserve what it has—whatever the cost."

But Applebaum's thesis doesn't explain why, in his view, conservatives have abandoned the attempt to persuade new populations. Applebaum himself acknowledges that a "conservatism defined by ideas can hold its own against progressivism, winning converts to its principles and evolving with each generation." Why, then, have conservatives supposedly given up?

The answer lies in a simple truth: Conservatives *haven't* despaired of winning over new converts. While a slight majority of Republicans believe that immigration should be reduced, pluralities or majorities of Republicans in the majority of polls believe that immigration is good for the country; a heavy majority of Republicans favor a "merit-based" immigration approach.

Conservative opposition to increased immigration isn't driven by fears of demographic change. It's driven by fear of *ideological change*. And that fear of ideological change is actually driven by Democrats' radicalism—and their overt suggestion that demographic change will provide the fodder for that radicalism. Applebaum rightly states, "The United States possesses a strong radical tradition, but its most successful social movements have generally adopted the language of conservatism, framing their calls for change as an expression of America's founding ideals rather than as a rejection of them." But today's successful social movements—the movements of the Democratic left—no longer bother with such niceties. Instead, they declare that America was, has been and always will be a racist place, riven by hierarchies of power, a corrupt structure to be overturned by that emerging demographic majority. These movements overtly call for curbing essential American freedoms—freedom of speech, freedom to bear arms, freedom of religion—in order to overthrow the corrupt power structure. The Democratic left then insists that immigration levels be increased both legally and illegally and suggests that its opponents are driven by unbridled racism.

In essence, the Democrats have decided that rather than expanding the application of American principles to new groups, they prefer to fundamentally *change* the definition of American principles and utilize immigration policy to facilitate that change. No wonder conservatives have responded by calling for immigration restrictions.

Conservatism must indeed root out and destroy any elements of race-driven policy from its midst. Conservatism speaks every language and can reside in any human heart. If the left wishes to avoid a civil war, it can start by doing the same: refraining from the argument that demographic change innately signals rewriting the definition of Americanism, and arguing in favor of that revision.

How to Disunite America

November 20, 2019

This week, Chick-fil-A, the immensely popular Christian-owned chicken sandwich giant, caved to the cultural left. For years, the left targeted Chick-fil-A, dating back to the 2012 revelation that Chairman and CEO Dan Cathy supports traditional marriage—and, horror of horrors, that charities given donations by Chick-fil-A support traditional marriage. This prompted paroxysms of outrage in the media, who quickly demanded that Chick-fil-A toe the Democratic Party line, despite the fact that then-President Barack Obama did not officially endorse same-sex marriage until May 2012.

The rage of the cultural left led to unsuccessful boycotts—Chick-fil-A's business expanded from $1 billion in 2001 to $5 billion in 2013 to $10.5 billion today—but successful hijackings of local government. When the cultural left can't achieve what it wants through public mobilization, it simply uses the power of government to blackmail those it dislikes.

So, despite the fact that Chick-fil-A had never discriminated against gay customers—it would sell a chicken sandwich to anyone—then-Boston Mayor Thomas Menino promised to ban the franchise from the city. Then-Chicago Mayor Rahm Emanuel quickly followed suit, pledging to support an alderman's plan to block Chick-fil-A from opening a restaurant at Chicago O'Hare Airport. San Antonio recently blocked Chick-fil-A from opening a restaurant at its airport, and the airport in Buffalo, New York, followed suit. San Jose, California, pledged not to renew Chick-fil-A's lease when it ran out.

Chick-fil-A has continued to receive blowback—and the blowback has widened, helped along by a hostile media. So Chick-fil-A decided to back down and announced publicly that it will no longer donate to traditional Christian charities such as The Salvation Army, the Fellowship of Christian Athletes and the Paul Anderson Youth Home. Chick-fil-A President and Chief Operating Officer Tim Tassopoulos explained, "as we go into new markets, we need to be clear about who we are."

Well, now they're clear. They're chickens.

Our First Amendment culture is endangered when local governments are given the capacity to block businesses from operating, not on the basis of business discrimination but on the viewpoint of the company's founders alone. That's precisely what's happening here. If giving to Christian charities now bars you from opening a restaurant at the airport, our culture is beyond the point of no return.

But there's something even more troubling going on here. In a free country, of course we get to choose which businesses to patronize. But is it *good for the culture* for us to segregate our business based on examining the politics of those who own our companies? Do we really want a country where we shop based on political affiliation? Where every decision, every day, is rooted in partisanship?

America's social fabric is already fraying. Politics has invaded everything from education to sports, from movies to fashion. Should politics now determine where we buy a chicken sandwich? A country that punishes restaurants because its founders don't openly celebrate same-sex marriage is a country destined to bifurcate. And that's pretty fowl.

Pete Buttigieg's Big Mistake: Telling the Truth

November 27, 2019

This week, South Bend, Indiana, Mayor Pete Buttigieg, who has risen to the top of the heap in early Democratic presidential primary polling in Iowa and New Hampshire, came under serious sustained attack for the first time in his candidacy. Buttigieg's early candidacy gained credibility thanks to the moderation he displayed compared with other Democrats. He quickly lost steam when he tacked to the left. Now Buttigieg has swiveled back toward the center, launching a series of assaults on the radical plans of Sen. Elizabeth Warren, D-Mass., and stealing her momentum in the largely white early primary states.

Normally, such political rises are attended by a spate of negative reactionary coverage, and Buttigieg's story is no different. The most effective attack on Buttigieg has centered around his complete lack of black support—a crucial problem for a candidate whose party sees black voters as a near supermajority of primary voters in states like South Carolina. Some of those attacks have focused on Buttigieg's less-than-stellar governance in South Bend, where crime rates have remained critically high and relations between the local population and police have been strained throughout his tenure.

But the latest attack is on Buttigieg's entire political mentality. This week, an article from Michael Harriot at The Root, titled "Pete Buttigieg Is a Lying MF," trended on Twitter. What, exactly, was

Buttigieg's lie? He suggested back in 2011 that not all educational outcome disparities between blacks and whites are attributable to systemic racism. "The kids need to see evidence that education is going to work for them," Buttigieg stated ("whitely," in Harriot's adjective). "(Y)ou're motivated because you believe that at the end of your educational process, there is a reward; there's a stable life; there's a job. And there are a lot of kids, especially the lower-income, minority neighborhoods, who literally just haven't seen it work. There isn't somebody they know personally who testifies to the value of education."

According to Harriot, this statement makes Buttigieg a "lying motherf-----." Why? Because majority-minority schools are underfunded compared with majority-white schools; because black students are "disciplined more harshly than white students," as Harriot says; because black college graduates don't have as successful an employment record as white college graduates. "Get-along moderates would rather *make s--- up* out of whole cloth than wade into the waters of reality," Harriot wrote. "Pete Buttigieg doesn't want to change anything. He just wants to *be something*."

But none of these three factors should explain the bulk of racial educational disparities. The black dropout rate from high school is far higher than that of white students, which has nothing to do with underfunded schools. Black students, by best available data, misbehave in school more often than white students. Black students drop out of college far more often than white students, which has nothing to do with institutional discrimination. Adjusting for household income, black women actually *overperform* white women in terms of college attendance and income. Something else is going on.

What is going on? According to a 2018 study from researchers at Stanford, Harvard and the Census Bureau, young black men do best in areas with high levels of fatherhood. Lack of school mobility, largely due to entrenched interests preventing such mobility, doesn't help either. Harvard's Roland Fryer formalized "a particular peer effect, 'acting white,' which potentially contributes to the ongoing puzzle of black underachievement." Former President Barack Obama similarly suggested an "element of truth" in the accusation that education is undervalued in many black homes, lamenting the attitude "OK, if boys are reading too much, then, well, why are you doing that? Or why are you speaking so properly?" A study from the Brookings Institution found that black students spend less time on homework than other racial groups—by a long shot.

So, is Buttigieg a "lying motherf-----" for pointing out that not all disparities can be attributed to institutional discrimination? Of course not. But in the Democratic Party, such common sense represents political suicide.

The Disproportionate Trickle-Down of Bad Social Politics

December 4, 2019

This week, Paul Krugman of The New York Times posited a theory: Red states cause depression and suicide. In a column titled "America's Red State Death Trip," Krugman wrote: "In 1990, today's red and blue states had almost the same life expectancy. Since then, however, life expectancy in Clinton states has risen more or less in line with other advanced countries, compared with almost no gain in Trump country. At this point, blue-state residents can expect to live more than four years longer than their red-state counterparts." On this basis, Krugman blasts Attorney General William Barr, who suggested earlier this year that militant secularism lies behind rising mortality in the United States. Instead, Krugman suggested that "these evils are concentrated in states that voted for Trump, and have largely bypassed the more secular blue states."

Krugman's analysis here is deeply flawed. It is flawed because it is far too simplistic. First off, states are not good proxies for political viewpoint *within states*, which would be far more telling: Texas encompasses both Austin and Lubbock, for example. Secondly, Krugman links 2016 voting patterns to 1990 data, but some of the states hit hardest by the opioid epidemic shifted over that same time frame from blue to red (e.g., Ohio, West Virginia and Michigan), demonstrating that voting may have resulted from distress, not the other wary around. But more importantly, Krugman assumes that conservatism presages lower life expectancy, rather than that those in lower-income rural areas are turning toward conservatism as a result of the social liberalism pushed forward by the left.

This analysis, as it turns out, is false. The reality is that broad trends over time point to the fact that low-income Americans have been disproportionately affected by the rise of social liberalism: the decline in religiosity, and the concomitant collapse of church and other social institutions have undermined precisely the same people who have been hit hard by the economy. Charles Murray pointed out this phenomenon in his book "Coming Apart" nearly a decade ago: America has bifurcated between more highly educated, higher-income Americans (Murray labels them residents of Belmont) and less educated, lower-income Americans (Murray labels them residents of Fishtown). This holds true regardless of race. And contrary to popular opinion, those who are less educated and lower-income, particularly in the white community—the base of support for President Donald Trump—have been disproportionately affected by the excesses of social liberalism. Between 1960 and 2010, the marital rate among Belmont whites ages 30 to 49 declined from 94% to 84%; the marital rate among Fishtown whites declined from 84% to 48%. Similarly, single motherhood increased from 1% of Belmont white college-educated women in 1970 to less than 6% in 2008; for Fishtown women, that number skyrocketed from 6% to 44%.

Most tellingly, secularism increased for both groups but far less among Fishtown residents (from about 29% in 1972-1976 surveys to 40% in 2006-2010 surveys) than Belmont residents (from 38% to 59%). In other words, the wages of social liberalism take a deeper toll on those who require more from social institutions, both economically and culturally. Denizens of The New York Times are far less likely to have children out of wedlock than the supposed religious fanatics they oppose—but they're also likely to push both governmental and social policy designed to promote single motherhood, for example. They don't pay the price of the policies they push.

Good decision-making and robust social institutions have a lot to do with life success. Promotion of bad decision-making and decay of key social institutions in the name of personal freedom may seem liberating to elitists like Krugman, but there are consequences for those who don't draw six-figure paychecks from Manhattan newspapers. Disdaining those who live in red states as victims of their own conservative backwardness isn't merely inaccurate; it's doubling down on stupid.

Will Democrats Accept the Results of the 2020 Elections?

December 11, 2019

In the lead-up to the 2016 election, Democrats fretted openly about the possibility that Donald Trump, being a rather poor sport, might refuse to acknowledge an election loss. To be fair, Trump refused to state that he *would* accept election results, depending on the circumstances: "I'll keep you in suspense," he stated in his Oct. 19, 2016, debate with Hillary Clinton. Clinton, for her part, called his statement "horrifying," adding that he was harming American democracy.

Trump, of course, won. And Clinton spent the next couple of years suggesting openly that she had been robbed in the election. Democrats blamed Clinton's election loss on Russian interference, on voter suppression, on anything but Clinton's campaign performance.

That wasn't a particular shock: After George W. Bush won the 2000 election, many Democrats continued to maintain that he was an illegitimate president. And not much changed in the nearly two decades since: In 2018, Democrats insisted that Georgia gubernatorial candidate Stacey Abrams had actually defeated Brian Kemp, despite having lost by approximately 55,000 votes. To this day, Democratic presidential candidates repeat the lie that Kemp stole the election from Abrams.

Now in the run-up to 2020, Democrats are already suggesting that if President Trump wins, the election will have been illegitimate. This time, they're pointing to Trump's supposed attempt to gather information from the Ukrainian government on potential 2020 rival Joe Biden in return for release of much-needed military aid. In fact, Democrats state that if Trump is not impeached, the 2020 results will inevitably be deemed improper.

On Sunday, Rep. Jerry Nadler, D-N.Y., who suggested way back in 2017 that though Trump was "legally elected," he was "not legitimate," doubled down: "The president, based on his past performance, will do everything he can to make it not a fair election. And this is part of what gives us the urgency to proceed with this impeachment." House Speaker Nancy Pelosi, D-Calif., said last week, "The president leaves us no choice but to act because he is trying to corrupt, once again, the election for his own benefit." Rep. Veronica Escobar, D-Texas, told CNN's Jake Tapper, "If you have a corrupt executive who is willing to maintain power by corrupting our election, there's an urgency there." Former federal prosecutor Anne Milgram wrote in The New York Times, "Who gets to pick the next president of the United States—President Trump, Ukraine, Russia or us?"

Impeachment, then, must be used *without proper evidence of a crime* in order to prevent Trump from stealing the election. By this logic, any suspicion of illegitimacy in an upcoming election becomes an excuse for ousting a legitimately elected president. This is a vicious cycle: illegitimate impeachments based on perception of illegitimate elections. And with Pelosi promising that our very civilization is at stake—a contention she made over the weekend—over the outcome of the next election, we can be sure that the pressure will continue to rise.

Things are already ugly in American politics. A republic can only be maintained when the people have faith that even if their side loses an election, that election was legitimate—and only when people believe that there is a tomorrow. With Democrats openly claiming that they can run an end-around with the electoral process because they don't trust the results, and stating that any future loss is evidence of corruption and a representation of the end of the country, things are about to get a lot uglier.

The Right to Destroy Cities

December 18, 2019

This week, the Supreme Court effectively mandated continued legal tolerance for homelessness across major cities on the West Coast of the United States. The 9th U.S. Circuit Court of Appeals recently ruled that Americans have a right to sleep on the streets, and that it amounts to "cruel and unusual punishment" under the Constitution to levy fines based on such behavior. That court—a repository of stupidity and radicalism, the Mos Eisley of our nation's federal bench—decided that writing a $25 ticket to people "camping" on the sidewalk is precisely the sort of brutality the Founding Fathers sought to prohibit in stopping torture under the Eighth Amendment.

That ruling was so patently insane that even liberal politicians such as Los Angeles County Supervisor Mark Ridley-Thomas joined the appeal attempt. "Letting the current law stand handicaps cities and counties from acting nimbly to aid those perishing on the streets, exacerbating unsafe and unhealthy conditions that negatively affect our most vulnerable residents," he explained.

But the 9th Circuit ruling will stand. That ruling followed a separate 2006 ruling from the same court, which found that cities could not ban people from sleeping in public places. In this case, Judge Marsha Berzon, in language so twisted it would make yoga pioneer Bikram Choudhury jealous, wrote that "the state may not criminalize the state of being 'homeless in public places'" and thus could not criminalize the "consequence" of being homeless.

It is worth noting that being homeless is not a "state" of being. It is not an immutable characteristic. It is an activity and can certainly be regulated. That doesn't mean the best solution is prosecution of those living on the street—a huge swath of homeless people are mentally ill or addicted to drugs and would benefit from better laws concerning involuntary commitment or mandatory drug rehabilitation. But to suggest that cities cannot do *anything* to effectively police those sleeping on the streets is to damn those cities to the spread of disease, the degradation of public spaces and an increase in street crime.

Hilariously, Berzon contended that this 9th Circuit ruling would not mandate cities to provide full housing to the homeless; it would just prohibit them from moving or arresting the homeless for living on the streets. Which is somewhat like Tom Hagen telling Jack Woltz that while he doesn't *have* to cast Johnny Fontane in his new war film, he can't stop the Corleones from rearranging the family stable.

But here's the problem: Cities that have attempted to provide increased housing for the homeless, despite some early successes, have seen their problems return. Cities like Seattle and Los Angeles have attempted to build new housing. It's been an expensive failure. It turns out that the carrot of housing must be accompanied by the stick of law enforcement. If you cannot compel drug addicts to enter treatment, or paranoid schizophrenics to take their medication, or those who refuse to live indoors to do so, homelessness will not abate.

As it is, the Supreme Court has damned America's major cities to the continuation of the festering problem of homelessness. And that problem won't be solved by judges who attempt to force social policy through deliberately misreading the Constitution, or who believe they are championing "freedom" for tens of thousands of Americans who are seriously mentally ill or addicted to drugs.

About the Author

Ben Shapiro was born in 1984. He entered the University of California Los Angeles at the age of 16 and graduated summa cum laude and Phi Beta Kappa in June 2004 with a Bachelor of Arts degree in Political Science. He graduated Harvard Law School cum laude in June 2007.

Shapiro was hired by Creators Syndicate at age 17 to become the youngest nationally syndicated columnist in the United States. His columns are printed in major newspapers and websites including The Riverside Press-Enterprise and the Conservative Chronicle, Townhall.com, ABCNews.com, WorldNetDaily.com, Human Events, FrontPageMag.com, and FamilySecurityMatters.com. His columns have appeared in The Christian Science Monitor, Chicago Sun-Times, Orlando Sentinel, The Honolulu Advertiser, The Arizona Republic, Claremont Review of Books, and RealClearPolitics.com. He has been the subject of articles by The Wall Street Journal, The New York Times, The Associated Press, and The Christian Science Monitor. He has been quoted on "The Rush Limbaugh Show" and "The Dr. Laura Show," at CBSNews.com, and in the New York Press, The Washington Times, and The American Conservative.

Shapiro is the author of best-sellers "Brainwashed: How Universities doctrinate America's Youth," "Porn Generation: How Social Liberalism Is Corrupting Our Future," and "Project President: Bad Hair and Botox on the Road to the White House." He has appeared on hundreds of television and radio shows around the nation, including "The O'Reilly Factor," "Fox and Friends," "In the Money," "DaySide with Linda Vester," "Scarborough Country," "The Dennis Miller Show," "Fox News Live," "Glenn Beck Show,"

"Your World with Neil Cavuto," "700 Club," "The Laura Ingraham Show," "The Michael Medved Show," "The G. Gordon Liddy Show," "The Rusty Humphries Show," "The Lars Larson Show," "The Larry Elder Show," The Hugh Hewitt Show," and "The Dennis Prager Show."

Shapiro is married and runs Benjamin Shapiro Legal Consulting in Los Angeles.

Catastrophic Thinking
is also available as an e-book
for Kindle, Amazon Fire, iPad, Nook and
Android e-readers. Visit
creatorspublishing.com to learn more.

o o o

CREATORS PUBLISHING

We publish books.
We find compelling storytellers and
help them craft their narrative,
distributing their novels and collections
worldwide.

o o o

Printed in Great Britain
by Amazon